PRAISE FOR PEACE SKILL

"A must for people who want to be change agents in society. Addresses transformation of conflict from an empowerment perspective."—Craig Arendse, director of mediation and transformation practice, Cape Town, South Africa

"Offers a ray of hope for individuals and communities who long for peace and reconciliation."—Dr. G. Douglass Lewis, president, Wesley Theological Seminary

"JUSTPEACE chose this manual as its primary training text. . . . There is none better!"—Tom Porter, executive director, JUSTPEACE, United Methodist Church

"Peace Skills worked for me as a participant, and I depend on the Manual and Guide as a trainer."—Dr. William O'Brien, founding director, Global Center, Samford University and training coordinator for Birmingham Civil Rights Institute

"Enables individuals to engage conflict in a truly transformative manner. . . . The skills have proven effective in the formation of multicultural teams." —Michael Mata, director, Los Angeles Urban Leadership Institute and professor, urban studies, Claremont School of Theology

"This guide reminds us of the basic things we tend to forget: how to listen, how to be empathic to others, and how to see things from the perspective of others."—Christine Loh, member of Parliament and founder, Citizens Party in Hong Kong, China

"In Indonesia there is a great need to empower people for reconciliation. *Peace Skills* is just what we need. I have used the Leaders' Guide and

Manual in my training workshops at our center for Reconciliation and Peace and will use the Indonesian language translation even more."—Judo Poerwowidagdo, president, Krida Wacana University, Jakarta, Indonesia

"Invaluable resource . . . artfully blends 'the basics' with advanced approaches . . . beneficial to both first-time learners and experienced practitioners."—Dr. John Paul Lederach, professor, Conflict Transformation Program, Eastern Mennonite University

"The focus on community transformation and self-conscious reliance on spiritual and moral resources made the peace skills material distinctive. "
—Dr. Thomas Hoyt, Bishop of CME church and former professor of New Testament at Howard University, ITC, and Hartford Seminary

"Our training has allowed Jacksonville to address issues in education, housing, and the environment. The program has equipped more than five hundred Jacksonville leaders to be agents of community transformation and has improved the quality and ownership of important public policy decisions."
—Bill Scheu, lawyer and community leader, Jacksonville, Florida

PEACE SKILLS

LEADERS' GUIDE

Alice Frazer Evans and Robert A. Evans
with Ronald S. Kraybill

JOSSEY-BASS
A Wiley Company
San Francisco

Library of Congress Cataloging-in-Publication Data

Evans, Alice F., date
    Peace skills leaders' guide / Alice Frazer Evans and Robert A. Evans with Ronald S. Kraybill.—1st ed.
        p. cm.
    Includes bibliographical references and index.
    ISBN 0-7879-4800-4 (alk. paper)
    1. Negotiation—Study and teaching. 2. Mediation—Study and teaching. 3. Conflict management—Study and teaching. I. Evans, Robert A., date . II. Kraybill, Ronald S. III. Title.
    BF637.N4 E93 2000
    303.6'9—dc21   00-11143

PB Printing   10 9 8 7 6 5 4 3 2 1

FIRST EDITION

CONTENTS

ACKNOWLEDGMENTS

AS AUTHORS we are indebted to the many co-trainers, workshop participants, and program members who gave time, energy, and wisdom to developing these resources for reconciliation and transformation. The Leaders' Guide is dedicated to those friends and colleagues in gratitude for their devotion to peace and justice.

The members of the U.S.-based Christian leaders Empowering for Reconciliation with Justice (CERJ) program call for special recognition. Forty already overextended pastors and lay leaders trained for two years to develop multiethnic teams of mediators, trainers, and advocates of community conflict transformation. These teams in Los Angeles and Philadelphia have committed themselves to an additional three years as volunteer community peacebuilders. Much of the material in the *Peace Skills* Manual and this Leaders' Guide was tested and revised in the CERJ workshops. This material was also used in workshops with groups of civic and religious leaders in dozens of communities in North America, Africa, and Southeast Asia.

We deeply appreciate the financial support for curriculum development for community conflict transformation from the Pew Charitable Trusts, the Ford Foundation, the W. K. Kellogg Foundation, the James Irvine Foundation, the William and Flora Hewlett Foundation, the Cuesta Foundation, the E. Rhodes and Leona B. Carpenter Foundation, and the John D. and Catherine T. MacArthur Foundation.

The board of directors of Plowshares Institute provided constructive critique and unstinting support of this decade-long research and writing process. Our partners in peacebuilding on the staff of Plowshares Institute, Bill Helmstetter, Janet Kochanowski, and Margaret Steinegger-Keyser, assisted in the preparation, testing, distribution, and seemingly hundreds of revisions of both the Manual and the Leaders' Guide with perseverance and good humor.

We are deeply indebted to our friend and dialogue partner, Walter Wink, for his liberating insight and unfailing ability to challenge and enrich our perceptions. Without the vision and commitment of Ron Kraybill, we would not have been so involved in a network of reconciling and transforming relationships, which creatively disrupted and profoundly enriched our lives. A significant portion of our workshops is based on skills and training exercises we learned from Ron and adapted for our work in North American cities and international settings. Although we take final responsibility for the content of this Leaders' Guide, we acknowledge the many contributions of our collaborator and friend to this volume. We are grateful to Sarah Polster, our editor at Jossey-Bass, for her persistence and flexibility on this project and to Michelle Moore for her editing contributions.

We firmly acknowledge the grace and presence of a God of Justice and Peace who makes all of this possible.

November 2000   Alice and Bob Evans
Simsbury, Connecticut

INTRODUCTION

FOLLOWING A SERIES of bitter confrontations between police accused of using excessive force and members of a poor inner-city neighborhood, local religious leaders began meeting on a regular basis with the mayor. They initiated a series of workshops on joint mediation skills training for law enforcement, city administrators, and community, religious, and business leaders. New, constructive, multi-ethnic coalitions began to emerge, including a joint African American–Hispanic economic project. Six months later, twenty-six of the forty-six community leaders who attended the first conflict transformation workshop returned for a full day of advanced skills training, offering their support and endorsement for additional community workshops.

• • •

The commander responsible for closing a U.S. military facility sought advice on managing the transition from the director of the area community council, which had recently sponsored a series of conflict transformation workshops. The director invited selected base personnel, community leaders, and the commander to an informal gathering at the community center. The meeting began with introductions and conversations in an informal setting; a sharing of common concerns followed. The group then requested that several additional meetings be facilitated by volunteer mediators who were trained in the earlier workshops. Six weeks later, while community negotiations at many other U.S. military bases slated for closing were being conducted in the presence of armed guards, base personnel and members of this community were gathering for potluck suppers and picnics before constructively discussing serious issues of toxic waste and land access.

These true illustrations come from different settings and involve different constituencies. What they have in common are the volunteer community peacebuilders who used the same training materials to build mediation skills, self-confidence, and community networks. This Leaders' Guide and the accompanying *Peace Skills* Manual constitute the concrete approach used in workshops in these and many other communities in North America, Africa, and Asia.

The *Peace Skills* Manual and much of the Leaders' Guide share a common history. Between 1990, when Nelson Mandela was freed from prison, and 1994, when the first "all-race" elections were held, South Africa faced significant social and political unrest. Even though the legal pillars of apartheid were falling, it was unprecedented for a ruling minority government to cede power to an oppressed people without bitter confrontations. As violence between and within communities escalated, trusted pastors, priests, and other local leaders were called on to mediate and negotiate disputes, but few had the basic skills or confidence to respond to these urgent requests.

A number of religious leaders, supported by the business community, acknowledged the need to develop a constructive approach to deal with inevitable conflicts. They joined others, including professional trainers in mediation, negotiation, and peacemaking, to form a cross-cultural partnership titled Empowering for Reconciliation with Justice (ERJ).

For three years, ERJ held national and local workshops throughout South Africa and trained over thirteen hundred political, religious, community, and youth leaders in basic mediation, negotiation, and proactive peacemaking skills. More than forty of those who received basic and advanced training taught hundreds more in workshops sponsored by other organizations. South African leaders such as Dr. Stanley Mogoba, then presiding bishop of the Methodist Church in Southern Africa and co-chair of the National Peace Accord, cite ERJ as a significant contributor to the slow but steady move from an ethos of violence and confrontation to one of negotiation.

In late 1994, many who participated in ERJ seminars were interviewed and asked to reflect on the most important aspects of their training. The surprising similarity of their responses led to the creation of standard goals and guidelines for future workshops. Since then, core components focusing on mediation skills have been introduced in many other countries, including Canada, China, Indonesia, the Czech Republic, Jamaica, Uganda, Zimbabwe, and the United States. Religious and community leaders involved in similar training in many parts of the world facing social change have also affirmed the validity of these guidelines.

A number of refinements have been made to the initial training materials, and the format has been adapted to meet the needs of local settings.

However, the guidelines have remained the same and continue to form the foundation of the present workshops.

GUIDELINES FOR COMMUNITY CONFLICT TRANSFORMATION WORKSHOPS

Although these community conflict transformation (CCT) training materials can be used in a variety of settings, they were developed with a clear set of guidelines to meet specific goals.

Designed for Active Community Leaders

CCT workshops are primarily intended to empower trusted local leaders with basic mediation skills and to develop volunteer networks of competent, proactive leaders who are committed to building and sustaining just and peaceful communities. The workshops are not designed for people seeking to become professional mediators or negotiators.

Designed for a Diverse Community of Participants

The greatest benefit of the workshops comes from the experience of unity in diversity. Participants are diverse in race, ethnicity, gender, age, and worldview, but they are united in their vision for working together to achieve greater understanding and respect. During the workshops, positive mutual experiences break down stereotypes and initiate personal relationships that build cross-cultural bridges.

Focused on Peacebuilding and Conflict Transformation

The *Peace Skills* Manual and Leaders' Guide affirm the importance of addressing immediate and urgent issues of conflict through a process often called *peacemaking*. This process usually involves an independent outsider or a balanced team of insiders who intervene when the parties are unable to resolve their conflict. Mediation is one of the peacemaker's most valuable tools. In addition to immediate intervention, CCT workshops also seek to build the capacity of community leaders to analyze conflict, to address the underlying causes of conflict, and to help them find ways to use the vast energy of conflict for constructive purposes—for conflict transformation. This is the long-term process we call *peacebuilding*.

The workshops enable a diverse group of community leaders to begin building sustainable relationships, promote cooperation, and identify ways to address unjust systems and structures. As peacebuilders, they can use mediation to enable conflicting parties to understand one another better—

to transform their relationship—and to empower them to identify and address the causes of their own conflicts. A critical mass of citizens committed to becoming peacebuilders can transform community conflicts into opportunities for positive systemic change.

Based on Experiential Teaching and Learning

The workshops rely heavily on locally relevant case studies and role-plays to draw on the diverse experiences and insights of the participants. Participants re-create the realities of real-life practice and learn to draw on their own inherent skills. In joint reflection, they evaluate together the most effective ways to deal with conflicts in their own communities.

Based on Moral, Spiritual, and Cultural Values

Many peacebuilders draw on deep moral, spiritual, and cultural values to motivate and sustain their work. They also believe it is ultimately the power of God and not human intervention alone that makes peace and reconciliation possible in divided communities. Some case studies and the text of the *Peace Skills* Manual and Leaders' Guide were designed to meet diverse needs of secular organizations and facilitators who work with public entities such as school boards or city councils. Other components, such as church-related case studies and sacred text studies, draw specifically on resources from religious and moral traditions. Nevertheless, all training materials are based on belief in the dignity of human life, respect for the needs of others, and responsibility for one's own actions. These moral and spiritual values are consistent with Christian, Jewish, Muslim, and Buddhist mandates and have built bridges in community conflict transformation workshops from Johannesburg to Jacksonville to Jakarta.

Designed for Sharing

The final workshop guideline is to empower participants to share basic skills and approaches to peacebuilding with their constituencies. We therefore encourage workshop leaders to share case teaching notes, role-play texts, and other teaching aids with participants after the workshop and to direct them to the numerous practice exercises on mediation skills in the *Peace Skills* Manual. Also, because the most effective workshops build on one another, leaders should recruit skilled participants in one workshop to serve as coaches and then as co-trainers in future workshops.

This last guideline underscores the primary goal of the Leaders' Guide: to offer suggestions and provide tools for local leaders to equip their communities with skills for peacebuilding.

IDENTIFYING THE BEST WORKSHOP FACILITATORS

Workshop leaders do not need to be professional mediators or conflict resolution trainers. The Leaders' Guide and *Peace Skills* Manual are written so that any skilled leader or trainer can study the curriculum and conduct a productive workshop. Effective workshop leaders should possess qualities similar to those of effective peacebuilders: sensitivity to others; awareness of social and cultural influences on one another's assumptions; the ability to listen deeply and with empathy, self awareness, open-mindedness; and the ability to draw on spiritual, moral, and cultural resources to shape values and sustain commitment.

Good workshop facilitators should also have a comprehensive understanding of the *Peace Skills* Manual, a commitment to study the Leaders' Guide, a solid understanding of adult learning, the self-confidence to adapt workshop designs to the teaching context, and belief and trust in each participant's capabilities.

TEACHING SKILLS AND APPROACHES

When adults in several workshops were asked to describe their "best teachers," almost all cited similar characteristics: teachers who had broadened their insights, challenged their assumptions, and pushed them to grow. These teachers also cared about their students, valued students' life experiences, and acknowledged their innate abilities.

This Leaders' Guide offers a variety of tools and teaching approaches to help workshop leaders become "best teachers." Discussions and exercises are specifically designed to draw on the participants' experiences and to sharpen their skills and abilities as mediators and peacebuilders.

Training in Multicultural Settings

Conflicts and ways of addressing them are heavily influenced by culture. Factors that lead to conflict in one culture may be ignored in another, or a problem-solving process that works well in one culture may be totally inappropriate in another. Increasing numbers of people from different cultures are living and working together throughout the world. When their traditional or cultural patterns of dealing with conflict are not compatible, the potential for misunderstanding is greater, and resolving conflict is more difficult. Therefore, a primary role of conflict transformation workshop leaders or facilitators is to develop a learning environment where participants can learn from one another as they analyze conflicts from different perspectives and discover the most effective responses to them for their communities. John

Paul Lederach, a noted mediation trainer, has termed this approach *elicitive* training.[1] Elicitive training, he says, differs significantly from *prescriptive* training, which assumes that the teacher is the expert and is responsible for transferring knowledge to an uninformed learner.[2]

Emphasizing an Elicitive Approach to Teaching

The workshop designs include a variety of ways to create an elicitive or shared learning environment in which teachers and students combine their wisdom and experience as co-learners:

- Individual reflection allows participants to identify their own conflict situations and explore their personal reactions to them.

- Group analysis of conflicts and the development of creative alternatives enable participants to share distinct cultural perspectives.

- Small group role-plays and discussions provide opportunities for constructive feedback and self-reflection.

- Sacred text studies enable participants to share spiritual and moral resources and connect their values, questions, and experiences to the task of building peace with justice.

While preferring this style of teaching, we acknowledge that it is also important for workshop leaders to take responsibility for providing structure and introducing new information to students.

COMMUNITY CONFLICT TRANSFORMATION IN PRACTICE

Rapidly changing communities across the world experience conflict around issues of economic disparity, race, culture, ethnicity, and religion. In such situations, trusted community leaders are often expected to be able to address community problems constructively. The *Peace Skills* Manual and Leaders' Guide offer tools and a process for sensitive and committed civic and religious leaders to build more just and peaceful communities.

At the time of this publication, more than sixteen hundred community, government, business, and religious leaders in ten U.S. pilot cities, from Hartford, Connecticut, to Los Angeles, California, have participated in community conflict transformation workshops. As a result, networks of local leaders have formed multiethnic teams to build bridges between their constituencies and to work together to address community problems. Some of these cities now have teams of volunteers mediating conflicts in issues ranging from loud radios to sex education in the public schools. In other U.S. cities, volunteer trainers are equipping neighborhood groups with mediation skills. In one city, more than five hundred citizens have been trained in basic CCT skills. Many participants attest not only that this proactive approach to conflict improves their communities but also that the workshop itself was a transformative experience.[3]

HOW TO USE THE LEADERS' GUIDE

This Leaders' Guide contains information workshop leaders will need to conduct a community conflict transformation workshop. It does not repeat material from the *Peace Skills* Manual but does give cross-references to relevant sections of the Manual. Facilitators should be well acquainted with the content of the Manual before presenting the basic workshop.

The Leaders' Guide is divided into three sections.

Section One, "Facilitation Skills," gives suggestions for using the workshops' primary teaching tools: role-plays, case studies, and sacred text studies. It also contains guidelines for selecting appropriate case studies and provides creative hints on leading different types of group discussions.

Section Two, "Workshop Designs," is the heart of the Leaders' Guide. Chapter Four outlines the basic CCT workshop and provides exercises for introducing concepts and skills of conflict transformation to civic and religious leaders. Suggested times to devote to each segment are indicated. The basic workshop design is parallel to the content of the *Peace Skills* Manual.

Chapter Five presents designs for half-day and one-day introductory workshops, which are often used to develop interest in conflict transformation. Portions of these shorter workshops are drawn from the basic workshop. Chapter Six describes advanced workshops, designed for participants who have completed the basic workshop.

Section Three, "Community Conflict Case Studies, Role-Plays, and Sacred Text Studies," provides full texts of the teaching tools described in Section One. Chapter Seven contains the full texts of case studies along with teaching notes and role-plays drawn from the cases. Chapter Eight contains independent role-plays for the basic workshop and the half-day introductory workshop.

Chapter Nine includes study guides for sacred texts selected from the Christian New Testament, the Hebrew Scriptures, the Muslim Qur'an, and a civic moral text from South Africa. The texts are organized thematically to match different components in the workshops and have a broad range of applications. Sample discussion questions, application to life exercises, and a historical background accompany each passage.

The easel icon throughout the *Leaders' Guide* indicates materials that may be prepared in advance of the workshop.

The Jossey-Bass Web site (www.josseybass.com/peaceskills) contains additional case studies, sacred text studies, suggestions for addressing community conflicts, and an extensive list of additional resources.

You may wish to read through the complete Leaders' Guide to gain a comprehensive view of the resources it contains and how they are interrelated. However, you may also choose to go directly to a particular section because you know your audience and you have a specific goal. You may then decide to select a portion of the basic workshop or combine several exercises from the Guide to share with your audience. For example:

- If you have two hours to help a group of city leaders or members of a religious congregation learn more about analyzing group conflicts, you may decide to select and teach one of the case studies in Chapter Seven.

- If you are asked by a group of young people to help them improve their listening skills, you could teach the section on paraphrasing in the basic workshop, Day One.

- If you are working with a faith-based group on improving multicultural communication, you may decide to combine a sacred text study of Luke 10: 25–37 about the compassionate Samaritan (see the Jossey-Bass Web site, www.josseybass.com/peaceskills) with the exercise titled "Building Cross-Cultural Understanding" described in the advanced workshop in Chapter Five.

Once you gain a grasp of the resources the Leaders' Guide offers, the combinations of case studies, role plays, sacred texts, and approaches to teaching a variety of mediation skills are limited only by your creativity.

PEACE SKILLS

LEADERS' GUIDE

Section One

Facilitation Skills

Near the conclusion of a community conflict transformation workshop, the thirty-five participants were asked how they planned to use their new skills or insights. Many people responded with concrete examples such as using paraphrasing in their workplace, more objective analysis of existing conflicts, and deepening cross-cultural alliances initiated in the workshop. Almost half of the participants also declared that one of their primary goals was to share what they learned with colleagues in their congregation, workplace, or community group. One noted that learning to use the energy of conflict to build relationships and move toward constructive change was as important for the city as the development of mediation skills for its leaders. This group of potential trainers, plus participants from two subsequent local workshops, met for a day-long "training of trainers" based on material in the Leaders' Guide. The group also planned future meetings for mutual support and to share with one another what they learned from joint and individual teaching experiences as they sought to transform the ethos of their city.

The Leaders' Guide is designed to help committed community leaders and group facilitators such as these conduct a wide variety of conflict transformation workshops, ranging from half a day to a full week, in a variety of settings. Section One focuses on the specific skills and approaches needed to most effectively use the teaching tools of role-plays, case studies, and sacred text studies. This brief introductory section reminds workshop leaders of basic facilitation skills and teaching approaches that leaders will need throughout the stages of any workshop—from long-range planning to evaluation. The following suggestions will help an individual workshop leader, but they are specifically intended for a team of facilitators.

Tools for Good Teaching: Long-Range Planning

- Learn as much as possible about the group's composition, size, and expectations before the workshop. The level of literacy, cultural or ethnic diversity, the need for translators, hearing or sight needs, handicapped access, and the participants' knowledge of one another will affect the pace, style, and content of the workshop.

- Develop overall workshop goals with the host or coordinator. Then, as a leadership team, select workshop components that will best meet these goals. Team members should also consider their own personal goals, such as listening carefully or not speaking too much, and share them with one another for support and accountability.

- Be realistic about goals and timing. Keep in mind that the size and nature of the group will determine how long a section will last. Select one or two workshop portions that you can omit if time does not allow you to do them well.

- Be clear about the purpose and content of each segment of the workshop. Leaders who are less familiar with mediation concepts should carefully study the parts of the *Peace Skills* Manual that correspond to components in the workshop design.

- Identify creative ways to form diverse groups for role-plays and exercises.

- Prepare several short group games or active songs that different leaders can use when group energy flags.

- Be clear with one another about the workshop's leadership style. Focus on an elicitive approach to the material.

- Plan for a relaxed, safe, and enjoyable environment where people can learn about themselves and from one another. Identify relevant examples from your own experience to personalize your teaching, and be ready for opportunities to invite participants to share their own experiences that relate to topics of discussion.

Tools for Good Teaching: Details Before the Workshop

- Request or gather supplies such as easels, flipcharts, colored markers, and masking tape. Prepare newsprint or posters for presentations of workshop goals, schedules, and specific skills like paraphrasing. Make sure there are large boards or wall space to post material so that it can be seen by all participants.

- Prepare name tags for workshop leaders and participants. Provide a sample if participants are to complete their own. Be sure name tags are legible from across the room.

- Plan the room arrangement. Because the workshop will be highly interactive, place chairs in a single semicircle, facing the most neutral or least distracting wall. Participants will then be able to see one another and easily engage in group dialogue. Avoid rows, tables, or desks if possible, as they can block interactivity and make small group formations more difficult.

- If possible, mail the selected case study and a copy of the handout "Problem-Posing Cases and How to Study Them" (Exhibit 2.1, appearing in Chapter Two), to participants before the workshop.

- Develop a concise evaluation form for participants to complete before they leave. Ask questions that will give information on what the leaders and hosts want to learn from the workshop. Open questions can include "What parts of the workshop were most helpful?" "What would you change?" "Which specific skills or insights about conflict transformation do you think you will use, and how will you use them?" You can also develop a form that combines open-ended questions with ones that rate workshop components on a numerical scale (1 to 5 or 1 to 7, for example).

Tools for Good Teaching: During the Workshop

- Establish a clear context for participants. Clarify the goals and schedule of the workshop, and share your expectations with the participants.

- Keep a clearly written, succinct record of group discussions. Writing in colored markers on newsprint is usually more visible than writing on chalkboards.

- Avoid covering completed newsprint pages. Many people remember what they see longer than what they hear. Therefore, post the pages around the room. They will be helpful during summary sessions and will provide a record of the content and progress of the workshop.

- Give clear directions, and make sure everyone is "on board" before moving on. Shouting directions at a dispersing group or speaking while passing out material is self-defeating.

- Be open to the possibilities of silence. Some of the best learning takes place in silent moments.

- In your interchanges with participants, model the kind of affirmative, constructive feedback that you want them to use with one another in debriefing role-plays.

- Resist the temptation to be the one with all the answers to questions about conflict situations. Redirect questions to the group, and encourage participants to share their own wisdom and experience so they can learn from one another.

- Be sensitive to the energy and interest levels of participants. Workshop designs seek balance by moving from presenting a problem or information to exercises to large and small discussions, but flagging energy or distractions may call for a creative change of pace or content. An observant leadership team member sometimes sees the need for a shift before the one who is in front. Therefore, make a team covenant of mutual support. Give permission to each other to intervene quietly if a leader is having difficulty or a contribution would enrich the discussion. A supportive relationship among leaders models the goals of the workshop.

- Build regular times for evaluation into the workshop. Take a few minutes at the end of each day for participants to give feedback about what they like about the workshop so far and what they would like to see improved. This builds a sense of group ownership in the workshop and models leadership based on principles of participatory peacebuilding. Plan regular times for the leadership team to meet and evaluate things as well.

CHAPTER 1

Using Role-Plays Effectively

ROLE-PLAYING is one of the most effective training tools for empowering participants. Unlike lectures or discussions, role-plays engage participants at every level—physical, intellectual, and emotional. Nobody falls asleep during a role-play!

Social scientists widely agree that it is more effective to focus on changing people's behavior than on changing their attitudes. People are remarkably capable of agreeing with new ideas that are presented convincingly while continuing to behave in the same old ways. Trying out new responses is a powerful strategy to help people break from destructive patterns of handling conflict. Role-plays offer an effective way to get people to try new responses, even if they are not yet convinced of the value of these responses in real life.

Role-plays also offer people an opportunity to practice and gain confidence in using new skills. Role-plays are a lot like flight simulations. They provide a safe place to practice new skills, where mistakes can be made without incurring major costs. And just as it takes a skilled flight instructor to design a safe and reliable simulation, a skilled workshop leader is needed to facilitate an effective role-play.

CREATING A SAFE SPACE

Engaging in role-plays, trying new behaviors, and exploring new ideas involve a great deal of risk. The risk is not necessarily physical or political, although those aspects may be a concern when adversaries are in the same

---

The suggestions for role-playing presented in this chapter were developed primarily by Ronald S. Kraybill.

workshop; it is rather the personal and social risk of embarrassment or failure. Many people avoid risk by maintaining control over their lives. Entering into role-plays requires a willingness to give up more control than many people are accustomed to.

Eagerness to learn makes most people willing to take the risks if they are in a positive and safe workshop environment. Such an environment does not happen by chance. It emerges through careful, constant effort on the part of the workshop leader or trainer, who has the greatest influence on the learning environment. From the beginning of the workshop to the end, the leader or leaders must model honesty, openness, modesty, fairness, emotional steadiness, and generosity of spirit to earn the trust of each participant.

Risk management is important to good training design. A good design begins with a relatively low risk level and gradually increases. Early exercises should involve everyone on equal footing, without calling on individuals to do unusual or difficult things in front of others. By the end of the workshop, individuals may be willing to try more challenging tasks as others observe.

Leaders can create a positive, safe environment by reminding the group that the workshop is a laboratory for learning, a place where people are expected to struggle and make mistakes. Do not criticize, and discourage others from being critical. Be on a constant lookout for opportunities to point out where participants are doing well. A positive learning environment makes participants more willing to experiment with new behaviors. Experiencing new behaviors frequently brings significant attitude changes as well. Participants often return months after attending a workshop to say, "That workshop changed my life." By trying out relatively simple new skills, they discovered new ways of relating to others and gained a new outlook on relationships and problems in their lives.

THE LEARNING CYCLE

The extensive use of role-plays and case studies in community conflict transformation (CCT) workshops is based on the belief that most people learn best when they are trying to address specific problems. The pattern for most sections of the workshops is to identify a problem, idea, or skill and then engage in an active learning exercise that calls on participants to respond to a problem, test an idea, or use a skill in the context of real-life conflicts. Participants do not need to fully understand a problem or master a skill at this point. The main objective is to engage them in a practical situation where they are challenged to use their abilities to respond to and experiment with possibilities.

The workshops are also designed to promote learning from participants. For this reason, the discussion period after a role-play, where group time is spent wrestling with a practical learning experience, is probably the most critical learning time in the workshop.

Think of the workshop as a series of repeated steps:

1. Input by the leader or a facilitated discussion of a particular problem or skill.

2. Role-plays in groups of three or four. Participants respond to a problem or use a skill that they discussed or saw demonstrated in the context of a real-life conflict.

3. Small group discussion about the role-play within each role-play group.

4. Large group discussion of issues that emerged in the small groups.

USING ROLE-PLAYS IN THE LEARNING CYCLE

Selecting the Place, Time, and Type of Role-Plays

One or more role-plays follows each case study in Chapter Seven. The role-plays begin at different points following the case events. Rather than beginning "cold" with a new context for each role-play, participants can continue to work with a situation they have already analyzed. This continuity gives realism to the mediation sessions and helps participants break down complex community problems into manageable parts.

In addition to "full" role-plays, which take the players through all four stages of mediation, several role-plays focus on practicing skills for particular stages of mediation. The workshop designs suggest appropriate places to use these role-plays.

Role-plays are also effective for introducing concepts or generating ideas. For example, a spontaneous role-play can introduce participants to skills and approaches to use in the challenging task of encouraging parties to agree to meet. Although this kind of role-play itself takes only a few minutes, the learning from a subsequent discussion can be significant.

Setting Up the Role-Play

Divide participants into small groups. One approach is to ask participants to stand in three even columns (four, if you use co-mediators). Those in the center column stay in place and identify one person on each side to form a team. The trainer can walk along the columns and check for gender, age, and ethnic balance on each team. Next, assign roles by columns. For example, assign the roles for the mediator to those in the center; identify those on the left as one party, and those on the right as the other party. Give participants time to read their roles. This process takes about ten minutes for a group of forty people.

In subsequent role-plays, ask those who have not played the mediator to stand in the center column. Some will be hesitant and may need encouragement to play the mediator at least once during the workshop. To help the participants empathize with others, tell them in advance which columns will be assigned to each party so that they may choose the role of a character they find hard to understand or one with whom they disagree.

To help participants play their roles more effectively, consider the following approach. After assigning roles and identifying teams, ask all those playing the mediator to get together and discuss various strategies, such as how they plan to open the conversation. Ask those playing the parties to meet in small groups—a different group for each party—to consider their primary concerns, important values, and mediation goals—what they hope to achieve in the meeting. This approach usually gives confidence to the mediators, but it can also be more challenging for them because it offers the parties a chance to become more deeply involved in their roles. Some trainers prefer to brief the parties orally in the belief that role-players do a better job when they are not referring to handouts. If you choose this approach, you can brief the parties during these separate meetings. Encourage them to take notes during the briefing to record key details.

Guidelines for Role-Playing

Before beginning the first role-play, share these guidelines with participants.

1. *Read your role only.* Do not discuss it with others until after the role-play.

2. *Read your assignment before the role-play begins.* Put it away, and act your part. Nothing kills the spirit of a role-play faster than having participants read their lines. (Trainer's note: Using the back of the role-play script as a name tag for parties and mediators limits dependence on the script and helps players enroll more quickly.)

3. *Do not overplay your role.* Play the part naturally, remembering that in real life people respond to what is happening to them. If your role briefing says you are angry, you don't have to stay angry. If something your mediator says or does has an impact on you, respond accordingly.

4. *Stay in your role.* If you make side comments or laugh "out of role," you break the dynamics of the role-play and reduce the learning potential for yourself and others. If you are stuck, call a timeout. Briefly discuss the situation, and quickly return to the role-play. You will learn more by trial and error than by lengthy discussions.

5. *Discuss the role-play with others in your small group.* Debriefing or discussing the mediators' work immediately after a role-play, pointing out what they did well and offering suggestions for improvement, can be the most important learning time in the workshop. The parties have a special role here in helping the mediators analyze the experience.

Co-Mediation in Role-Plays

Although some role-plays in the Leaders' Guide are specifically designed for two parties and a single mediator, encourage people to co-mediate with another participant when possible. Co-mediation enables people to support one another in the early learning stages. Co-mediators can be important in building trust and addressing conflict in a diverse community. In a dispute between a young Hispanic man and an older Korean woman, for example, a solo mediator is likely to be viewed with some skepticism by at least one of the parties. Co-mediators of different gender and ethnic or cultural identity can reduce this danger.

It is important for co-mediators to get together and plan their approach before beginning a session. Suggest that they mediate in "chapters," alternating leadership for each chapter. As familiarity with the process improves, co-mediation rapidly gets easier, and the need to take turns diminishes. Discuss with participants the advantages and disadvantages of having a team of mediators. A description in the *Peace Skills* Manual (Chapter Three, "Mediation: A Tool for Empowering Others") lists points raised by previous groups and offers additional suggestions for co-mediation.

DEBRIEFING ROLE-PLAYS AND USING COACHES WITH SMALL GROUPS

Debriefing role-plays is as important as practicing new skills and behaviors. If the workshop leader gives clear instructions and participants reflect critically on the role-plays, they will learn much from one another.

The task of the parties is not only to act an assigned role but also to offer constructive feedback at the close of the role-play. Leaders should alert the parties before beginning the role-play that they will be responsible for creating a safe learning place for their mediator in the debriefing.

Guidelines for Debriefing in Small Groups

The following suggestions can increase the usefulness of debriefing. Share these suggestions with the workshop participants before they begin the small group debriefing of their first role-play.

When Giving Feedback ...

1. Begin by reflecting on what the mediator did well. Most learning mediators feel overwhelmed by their task and are conscious only of their mistakes. They need the support of the parties to be reminded of their strengths. Hearing strengths pointed out makes people even more effective in using them in the future.

2. Discuss things the mediator found difficult. Focus on actions or techniques that can be altered: "It would have helped me to see our problems listed on the board."

3. Share specific instances in the role-play where the parties might have responded differently if they were the mediators. Offer concrete examples and use "I" statements in discussing them: "I learned the importance of holding to the ground rules. When Sarah broke them by interrupting me, I was afraid I wouldn't get a fair hearing."

4. Share general lessons learned from the role-play.

5. Allow someone receiving feedback to respond to your comments and "have the last word." Never give others feedback unless you are prepared to listen thoughtfully to their responses. Close on a positive note of affirmation.

6. Consider whether there are questions and concerns raised by the role-play you wish to raise during the large group discussion.

When Receiving Feedback ...

Receiving feedback gives an opportunity to practice the difficult but transforming art of nondefensiveness. The following suggestions may assist in this.

1. You are in a "learning laboratory." If you are not making mistakes, you may not be learning much.

2. Practice the art of devoting your attention to hearing and understanding feedback rather than on defending things you did. The feedback of those being "mediated upon" gives important information for your reflection.

3. It is better to learn from mistakes in a safe learning environment than when you are mediating "for real."

4. We are all responsible for our own learning. Take responsibility for your successes and your failures, and the workshop will be rewarding for you.

Using Coaches in Small Groups

Placing a "coach" in each small group can substantially enhance learning. Coaches do not have to be experts, but they must have some experience with mediation and understand the mediation process. Involving people who are in the process of learning mediation and who have been through the workshop previously is also a highly effective way to equip new trainers. To gain the greatest benefit from the experience, coaches should participate in designing and leading portions of the workshop as well.

More important than knowledge of the mediation process is the commitment of coaches to empowering workshop participants. Coaches, like trainers, face strong temptations to exercise power and show how much they know. They must be willing to serve as quiet, thoughtful servants of their small groups and assist group members to share among themselves. If coaches cannot accept this role and keep a low profile in the discussion, their presence is more destructive than helpful.

If possible, use one coach for each small group. Since the small groups change with each role-play, coaches will work with a different group each time a new role-play begins. During the role-play, coaches should be close to, but outside of, their small group circles. This will allow them to hear and observe without getting in the way of the role-players.

Tasks of Coaches

Coaches for small group role-plays have the following tasks:

Observing

Observe the group carefully during the role-play. Be fully aware of what is happening. Jot down mediators' approaches or skills that were either effective or blocked the discussion.

Supporting Constructive Role-Playing

Encourage constructive role-playing. Sometimes it is necessary to remind participants to "stay in role" or to discourage "overplaying" a role.

Assisting Struggling Mediators

Support the mediators in a low-key way if they are struggling. If they need help, consider the following interventions.

Passing notes. This enables input to the mediators without disrupting the flow of the role-play. Offer brief suggestions about skills or strategies. Preface suggestions by affirming something the mediators are doing well: "You are listening splendidly. Try being more firm about not allowing them to interrupt each other." Passing notes to the parties can be effective for dealing with problems such as overplaying or "moving out of role."

Joining the role-play as a mediator for a few minutes. Use this approach only if the mediators are really stuck. Floundering and making mistakes are part of learning and should not per se cause a coach to step in, but there is no point in allowing mediators to wallow endlessly if they are clearly beyond their ability to recover. If you choose to enter as a mediator, move to a position beside the mediators. Quietly enter the discussion as part of the mediation team. Steer things as you think they should go; then pass the initiative back to the other mediators, withdraw from the mediation role, and physically move outside the circle back to the observer role. Ideally, this takes no more than two to four minutes.

Calling a timeout. This is the most drastic intervention, for situations that seem beyond salvaging by other strategies. After halting the role-play, you can do any of the following:

- Ask the parties to give feedback to the mediators about what is happening or what they should do.

- Ask some or all of the role-players to describe what they think is happening.

- If the mediators are lost, have one of the parties change roles with a mediator.

- Offer suggestions to the mediators about what to do.

Keep the discussion short so that the group can return to the role-playing as quickly as possible. Focus on identifying options for moving the situation forward, and save in-depth analysis for the debriefing time at the end.

Facilitating Debriefing

When the role-play is finished or the workshop leader calls time, step in decisively and take charge of the debriefing. Use the following strategies to help people return to their "real" selves and feel OK about the role-play:

- Remove name tags worn for role-plays.

- Ask people to shake hands "back in real life now." They will invariably laugh, which is one of the fastest ways to come out of a role. Encourage good-natured laughter and humor throughout the discussion.

- Invite people to talk about "how you felt in your role." By expressing anger or frustration, people are able to separate the role-play from real life. Always allow people who had the toughest or most vulnerable role to speak first.

The major value of debriefing is for people to identify what they have learned from the experience. Begin by analyzing strengths before difficulties. Resist the temptation to put yourself, as trainer or coach, in the role of expert analyst. Let the role-players provide as much analysis and feedback as possible. You are an important resource, but your first commitment is to help the group members wrestle with the issues they encountered. Offer your own insights only after the group has a chance to respond or has specifically asked for ideas. If you are speaking more than one-third of the time, you are probably dominating the discussion.

Giving Feedback

Give individuals personal feedback whenever possible. Look for good skills, and point these out in the group discussions and in private. Give constructive criticism in small doses by suggesting "more of" or "less of" behaviors in question.

LEADING LARGE GROUP DEBRIEFING OF ROLE-PLAYS

Whenever possible, role-playing and small group discussions should be followed by a large group discussion facilitated by one of the trainers. This can begin in an empowering way if the leader of this discussion first asks for parties to describe a few things their mediators did that were effective. Alternatively, you can give mediators the opportunity to begin by sharing some of the things they did that worked best or were most helpful. Beginning on a positive note is an important way to build confidence and sets the stage for discussing more difficult issues that are likely to arise later. You can guide discussion into the terrain of difficulties by asking people to identify problems they encountered or to share things they learned from mistakes they made.

In addition to having participants discover answers to their own questions, another empowering strategy in facilitating a large group discussion is to look for opportunities to turn a theoretical question into a mini role-play. For example, if someone raises a question about dealing with interruptions, the trainer might ask if this was a problem that emerged in the last role-play. If so, the trainer can ask those who participated in the role-play to demonstrate what happened.

Have the role-play group give a five-minute replay of the problem without discussing how the mediators dealt with it. Then cut in and ask the full group, "How would you deal with this problem if you were the mediator?" Allow the group to discuss the problem or ask the role-players to demonstrate what they would do as mediators. Or you may allow the role-play to continue until the original mediators show how they tried to address the problem. This sets the stage for group discussion.

BEYOND THE ROLE-PLAY

Role-plays demonstrate some of the many steps in the long process of constructively addressing a community conflict. Workshop leaders should encourage participants to consider long-term implications when they discuss issues of justice and building sustainable peace in the conflict addressed in the role-play. Asking questions—"How could what happened in the role-play affect the overall situation?" or "What next steps could the parties take to address some long-term goals suggested in the case discussion?"—can help keep the workshop focused on the overall goal of realizing the potential for community transformation that comes from community conflicts.

CHAPTER 2

Case Studies in Conflict Transformation
What They Are and How to Use Them

ONE BRIGHT AUTUMN DAY a number of years ago, walking in a local neighborhood with our four-year-old son, Bob and I came to a yard filled with used toys. Allen immediately spotted a large red metal crane. It was old and rusty, but the crank still worked. The little boy picked up the toy with a great grin on his face, and we gladly paid the $1.00 tag sale price. Allen played in the garden with the crane the entire afternoon, explaining that he was "digging for dinosaurs."

By evening, he was covered with mud and rust. My only recourse was to bathe him before supper. I drew a tub full of warm soapy water, took off Allen's clothes, and went to lift him into the tub. He suddenly grabbed the crane, insisting that he "needed" to take the crane into the tub. As we argued, Allen began to cry, tears streaming down his grimy cheeks. I decided to use some good, maternal psychology and announced that I had just talked to the crane, and the crane didn't want to take a bath. Without blinking, this four-year-old looked up at me and said, "It's OK. I just talked to the crane's mommy, and she said he had to!"

Allen was calling on a different—and in his mind, a higher—authority! Those of us who teach call on a variety of authorities: a text, our education, our mentors, and so forth. Case teaching draws especially on the authorities of the wisdom and experiences of participants.

Good case teaching begins with the case experience, not with the teacher's theories or principles. For this reason, in contrast to a lecture, an authentic case discussion challenges case leaders to trust the participants' insights and life experiences. This approach helps a leader move from the role of teacher to that of "co-learner," a role that is particularly effective for teaching and learning in diverse groups. Co-learning gives participants of different gender, age, experience, and culture or ethnicity opportunities to share their perspectives and helps them gain a better understanding and a deeper appreciation for one another.

Case studies are learning tools that present stories of actual events and dilemmas faced by real people.[1] There are many ways to address the problems raised in a good case study. Case studies are particularly useful in workshops on community conflict transformation (CCT) because they can help a diverse group of participants become more creative in both analyzing and addressing community conflicts.

Why use written case studies rather than "the real thing"?

Community groups that initiate workshops on conflict transformation are often already involved in one or more areas of conflict where some community members have deep feelings of hurt and anger. Primary goals of the CCT workshop are skills training and developing participants' abilities to handle conflicts more constructively. Another goal is to bring together in a nonthreatening environment a diversity of participants, many of whom have quite different perspectives on current conflicts. Community members may disagree deeply about the "facts" of a local situation and find it difficult to openly state their views until trust has developed. Consequently, basic workshops use a case study that is relevant to the community but is safer than current community issues. The advanced training workshop takes participants who have already attended the basic training a step further to analyze and address conflicts in their own communities.

CASES IN COMMUNITY CONFLICT TRANSFORMATION

In the early 1990s, mediation and negotiation trainers in South Africa participating in the ERJ program began to adapt the case study approach to training in community conflict transformation. Rather than use cases written elsewhere, the trainers wrote cases about actual conflicts in South African communities. In so doing, they made a number of interesting observations:

- Group analysis of a case problem, particularly when groups were racially, culturally, and economically diverse, allowed participants to share their experiences and broaden their cross-cultural understanding.

- Group discussions helped participants develop conflict analysis skills by allowing them to sort out problems and identify factors that contributed to a particular conflict.

- Gathering data from a variety of sources about community conflicts became important for local leaders who often worked in isolation.

- Attempting to understand the various parties in case studies helped improve listening skills and break down stereotypes.

- Discussing strategies for resolution demonstrated the value of joint problem solving as participants developed suggestions that they would not have thought of on their own.

- Using case studies and drawing role-plays from them introduced important new learning opportunities into mediation workshops. Role-plays alone are inadequate to deal with issues of context and structural realities. Case study discussion *plus* role-playing enabled seamless integration of both analysis and skill into workshops.

The characteristics that made problem-posing case studies a valuable tool in helping South African community leaders become agents of reconciliation and transformation have proved equally effective in workshops in Asia, North America, and other parts of Africa.

SELECTING THE RIGHT CASE

The most gripping case for community leaders to analyze is usually the one they are dealing with at the moment. But discussing controversial issues may not be the most effective way to build networks across diverse constituencies and may distract from learning basic mediation skills in an initial workshop. In addition, the task of developing a new case can be daunting for workshop leaders. For these reasons, most facilitators begin with cases that have been tested and proved effective. However, it is important that facilitators select the most appropriate case study for their group. Even experienced case teachers do not always get it right. For example, one teaching team selected "Beyond the Battle" for a group of university faculty members. This case focuses on decisions that a troubled urban board of education had to make. Although the case had led to energetic discussions in previous community workshops, it was difficult for this group of faculty members from a small academic community to relate to the central problems or to understand the perspectives of the case characters. Class energy was low, and the role-plays seemed artificial.

In another situation, a community leader advised facilitators not to use the case study "Giving Thanks." This case study deals with a conflict between Korean American merchants and African American residents. In other settings, this case had proved to be an excellent one to help groups understand the impact of cross-cultural differences in community conflicts.

However, this leader pointed out that the case was similar to a recent unresolved incident in her community. She wisely advised that lack of trust among the participants could block their ability to discuss the case objectively. The workshop leaders chose another case.

In contrast, when the same leaders discussed topical issues of three different cases with a sponsoring church group, committee members selected "Prairie Storm" (available on the Jossey-Bass Web site, www.josseybass.com/peaceskills) because it raised issues similar to those in their congregation. They felt that discussion of this case would enable members of the congregation to deal "safely" with a potentially difficult topic and develop guidelines for handling similar conflicts.

These examples show the importance of looking carefully at participants and asking:

Which case issues will be most engaging for the group?

Will an ethnically or economically diverse group be able to identify with case characters and perspectives?

Because the basic workshop is not intended to deal with specific community problems, are there sensitive issues that should not be raised?

To select the most appropriate case, facilitators should assess the specific goals of the course and the group, identify primary issues the community currently faces, and gather beforehand as much information as possible about the nature and composition of the workshop participants. The synopsis of several cases, presented at the end of this chapter, should help facilitators consult with workshop sponsors and choose the best case.

PRESENTING THE CASE

There are a number of ways to introduce participants to a case study. Assigning readings before a workshop gives participants time to study the case carefully. Therefore, when possible, mail the case to participants before the workshop with a copy of Exhibit 2.1, "Problem-Posing Case Studies and How to Study Them." However, some people may not receive the case in time, and others may not be able to read it before the session. Because there are few teaching disasters that equal teaching a case study that participants have not read, give the group ten to fifteen minutes to read or review the case during the workshop session. Those who have previously read the case may be able to offer the most insightful comments, but at least everyone will be familiar with the text.

EXHIBIT 2.1

Problem-Posing Case Studies and How to Study Them.

There are many types of case studies. Some are brief, one-page descriptions of an encounter between two people. Others contain detailed, often long historical descriptions of a legal or business dilemma. The type of problem-posing case used in this workshop follows a model developed by Harvard Law and Business schools. These are carefully written descriptions of an actual situation or event. However, the persons and places in this type of case are usually disguised to protect the privacy of those involved in the situation.

The basic information that readers need to understand the situation is provided. Most problem-posing cases are seen through the eyes of one person who must make a critical decision. The case is usually open-ended, and readers are not told what decision was made. Information about the decision is balanced, and there is no obvious or "correct" answer. The work of discussion participants is to "enter" the experience of the decision maker, analyze the context and events of the situation, and suggest the best options for moving toward resolution. Participants should be able to suggest what information informs their analysis and to offer the reasons behind the alternatives they suggest.

SUGGESTIONS FOR STUDYING A CASE FOR GROUP DISCUSSION

A successful case discussion requires careful preparation and open interchanges between participants. The following steps will help you in sharing your insights and points of view.

1. Immerse yourself in the case; get to know the details. If possible, read the case several times.

2. Analyze the case after reading it.

    *   Write out the cast of characters.

    *   Develop a chronology of events in the case.

    *   Identify the basic issues (especially those things—acts, values, and attitudes—about which decisions need to be made).

    *   Try to see all the positions reasonable persons might take.

3. Mull over the case; that is, think about it casually. Let things flow through your mind.

4. Remember that there is usually no one "right" answer.

5. Participate in the discussion.

    *   Push your ideas; be willing to give reasons.

    *   Listen to others; evaluate their positions.

    *   Keep an open mind; be willing to change it upon new insights or evidence.

    *   Enjoy yourself!

Peace Skills Leaders' Guide by Alice Frazer Evans and Robert A. Evans with Ronald S. Kraybill. Copyright © 2001 by Jossey-Bass Publishers, San Francisco, CA.

These suggestions were adapted from material developed by M. B. Handspicker, Andover Newton Theological School.

You may also present a case by reading it aloud or by asking a group of preassigned readers and a narrator to "act out" the case. Although these approaches take more time, they are useful in special circumstances, such as when you are leading a group whose first language is not English, when some participants are visually handicapped, or when you are unsure of the participants' literacy level.

You might introduce a case study in the following way:

> The case we will be studying is true, although the place and the names of the people have been changed to protect their privacy. This type of case is like a good mystery. It has a dilemma, a cast of characters, and a plot. The primary difference is that the case has no "last chapter." We don't know what happened. The "last chapters" will be developed during our discussion, as each of you finds clues in the text that others may have missed. The goal of our discussion is not to arrive at one "correct" answer to the case problems. Our goal is to gather in a systematic way the most relevant clues, to analyze these clues responsibly, and to determine viable alternatives for positive resolution of the case.

READING THE CASE

After introducing the case, suggest that participants read or review the text using the following guidelines:

- Identify important information about the case context.

- Be clear about the sequence of events.

- Identify primary issues and characters.

- Try to understand the different perspectives each character brings to problems in the case.

- Begin to develop possible alternatives to resolve the case dilemma or dilemmas.

- Read with an open mind, and be prepared to share your insights with others and to listen to others.

- Be ready to have fun!

Before asking participants to read or review the case, it may be helpful for the facilitator to write the guidelines for reading and participating on newsprint. For easy reference by the group, the facilitator might also write on newsprint a brief summary of the points just given about the use of case studies, such as "True situation" and "No right answer."

TEACHING THE CASE

When teaching a case study, a case discussion leader must follow three important rules:

- Be very familiar with the case material.
- Make sure participants have sufficient time to read the case.
- Allow enough time for a good discussion.

Case discussions usually take sixty to ninety minutes, depending on the size of the group and the goals of the facilitator. A shorter time will not allow sufficient discussion, and most people cannot stay seated and focused for much longer.

A good conflict transformation case teacher asks a series of carefully designed questions and guides a constructive discussion so that all can learn from one another and be better equipped to face similar situations in the future.

A well-facilitated case discussion also provides a rich opportunity for a diverse group of people to come together, share their personal and cultural approaches to a specific conflict, and come to a better understanding of issues and different perspectives as they work together to resolve a problem. The primary tasks of the case teacher are to give structure and momentum to the discussion, challenge unrecognized assumptions or stereotypes, help participants hear one another, and enable them to grow in knowledge and skill through this shared experience.

Developing Goals and Teaching Approaches

Each case study in this guide is accompanied by "teaching notes" that suggest one of many ways to structure case discussion. You may adopt the goals suggested in these notes or develop your own. Whatever you decide, carefully consider in advance where you want your discussion to go in light of the issues you want raised and the needs and nature of the group you are leading. Prepare a simple, one-page teaching outline for quick reference during the teaching session, and keep your goals clearly in mind. Frame your questions in advance. Anticipate how members of your group might respond to each one, and be open to their creative insights. (The words and phrases in italics following questions on the teaching notes are not suggested "answers." They are responses that other groups have contributed and are included to help you anticipate how participants may respond.)

Setting the Stage

Place on several boards or newsprint the basic outline for the discussion, such as "Context and Issues" (on one easel or board), "Parties" (on at least two wide sheets of newsprint), and "Alternatives" (on another easel or board). Explain that the participants will be asked to analyze the causes of the conflict, to understand the persons involved, to focus specifically on reasons for the characters' different positions, and to discuss alternatives for the main characters.

Leading the Discussion

Although the order may vary, the primary components of most case teaching notes are context or setting, issues, persons, alternatives, and resources. These discussion sections are parallel to many components of addressing a community conflict: gathering information about the context and causes of the conflict, identifying the parties and stakeholders, looking beyond the parties' positions or demands to their needs and interests, developing goals and strategies for addressing the conflict, and identifying resources.

Context

A nonthreatening way to enter the discussion is to gather factual information about the case setting. For example, ask participants to quickly identify facts in the case that describe the community, organization, or congregation.

Issues

Once people are clear about the setting, deepen the discussion to draw out their analysis of the central issues raised by the case. In many teaching notes, issues are introduced by a discussion of the *causal or contributing factors* that led to the case conflict or conflicts. Ask participants to support their understanding of issues with data from the case. Be prepared for very different perspectives to be raised, particularly in a multicultural group.

Either during or after the discussion of the contributing and causal factors of the case conflict, use the acronym RIVIRS (Resources, Information, Values, Interests, Relationships, Structures) to help participants remember this tool for analyzing conflict situations (*Peace Skills* Manual, Chapter Two, "Understanding Conflict and the Role of Mediation"). Draw a big circle cut into six wedges, like a wagon wheel with six spokes, and in each wedge indicate a type of conflict, as shown in Figure 2.1.

Have the group distinguish specific areas where information—or misinformation—is a source of conflict in the case situation. Which resources are factors? What values are in conflict? This type of analysis helps make complex conflict situations more manageable. Note that each type of conflict calls for a different response by peacebuilders. Conflicts about information may be relatively easy to resolve, while conflicting parties may need to learn how to live with conflicts involving values.

FIGURE 2.1

Six Types of Conflict.

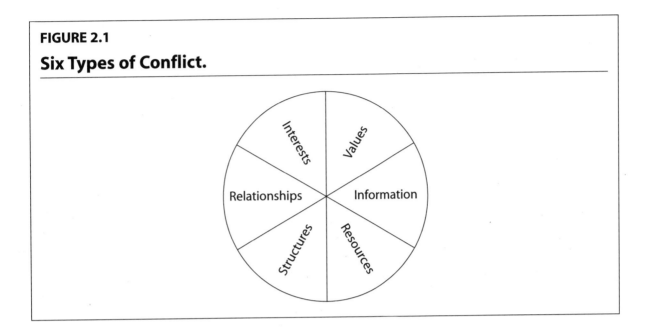

Persons: Parties and Stakeholders

(Review "Focus on Interests," particularly the section titled "Move from Demands to Interests," in Chapter Seven of the *Peace Skills* Manual.) Each set of teaching notes allots a significant block of time to discuss specific case characters. Before beginning this discussion, make a large chart (on the board or two sheets of newsprint) with four columns, headed "Person," "Position," "Needs/Interests," and "Feelings," and write the names of the primary case characters in the first column. A suggested sequence for discussing case characters follows.

1. Identify a specific character according to factual information presented in the case.

2. Identify the public position, if any, that the character takes on the selected issue.

3. Discuss the interests and needs that inform that position.

4. Consider what the character may be feeling about the situation.

In a community dispute, parties who take the same position often have different, even conflicting, reasons for doing so. Sensitivity and skill in moving the parties away from their demands to revealing their needs and interests are central to successful problem solving.

As you begin to discuss demands or positions, needs, and interests, the following simple illustration may be useful: The mother of a young child has taken a *position* and made a public *demand* that the city install a traffic light at a particular intersection. Her *interest* is that her son be able to cross the street safely on his way to school. Her *need* is to protect her child. If city leaders are able to see beyond her demand, they may be able to meet the mother's needs and interests by means other than a traffic light.

Move to "interests and needs" by asking questions such as "What is this person most concerned about?" or "Why do you think Michael Gonzales has publicly declared his position on the side of security when he also sees advantages in the reform package?" or "Why has Martha Jones not taken a public position on funding?" Remind participants that focusing on the demands parties make seldom leads to sustainable community dispute resolution. The seeds for mutually beneficial resolutions are found most often in common concerns that are revealed when parties identify and express their real needs and interests.

Asking participants to imagine what a specific case character is feeling not only helps them identify with the case character but also helps break down stereotypes. A discussion of their perceptions helps participants get in touch with their own prejudices and move beyond preexisting attitudes that can block their hearing of the needs and interests of particular parties.

An alternative approach to studying the characters is to assign each primary character to a small group that discusses the categories and "introduces" that person to the large group. Be sure to allow time for large-group discussion of each small group presentation.

Participants will disagree on interpretations of some characters. Encourage them to discuss their disagreements with one another, and ask them to refer to information in the case that supports their perceptions. Be on guard for stereotypes: "Sally Thompson is a rich white do-gooder who doesn't care about people in the city" or "Thomas Jackson is an angry black man who hates whites." Ask participants not to talk *about* the characters but to "get into their *feet*," identify with them, and try to understand the situation as the characters would. Explain that identification with other people is an indispensable part of being a sensitive and unbiased peacebuilder.

Do not forget to add the category of *stakeholders* to the discussion of persons. Stakeholders are groups or individuals who could have an impact on the situation but have not yet been identified as a "party" directly involved in the conflict. Stakeholders include persons or groups who could either block or become resources for resolving an immediate crisis or long-term issues facing a community.

While participants discuss the case characters, record information and issues in a visual form that can be saved for future reference in the workshop. For easier identification, use a different colored marking pen to record information about each character.

Alternatives

This section helps participants consider how a crisis can become a catalyst for constructive change. Dedicate enough time to develop short- and long-term goals and strategies for addressing the case conflicts. Discussions can be conducted in a plenary session or in small groups. Urge participants to be creative and concrete in their suggestions, drawing on their previous analysis of the conflict and the parties.

One approach to a full group discussion is for the case facilitator to sit in front of the group and enter the role of the primary character. Remind participants that real life usually requires a decision to be made. Ask them to telephone you with their advice. Respond as the character might by expressing concern, asking questions, and pushing for concrete suggestions ("I like your idea of postponing the vote. How do you propose I do that?").

An alternative might be to form groups of six to eight people. Ask half of the groups to determine short-term goals and specific strategies to address the immediate issues constructively. Ask the others to identify long-term goals and strategies to address systemic issues. They should consider the causes of the conflict identified earlier as they develop these goals and strategies.

If you use small groups, write group tasks on newsprint in advance for easy reference. Have each group list its suggestions on a single sheet of newsprint. Then, rather than asking for oral reports, have participants stand and read the posted goals and strategies of the other small groups.

Resources

Use this closing discussion to identify individual and community resources that could assist the case characters in reaching a just and sustainable resolution of the conflict. In the basic two-day workshop design, this discussion is held after a break and focuses on identifying the skills or personal resources of an effective community facilitator. This discussion leads into the workshop session on listening skills and paraphrasing.

ADDITIONAL SUGGESTIONS FOR EFFECTIVE CASE TEACHING

The following suggestions will help maximize case discussions.

Transitions

One way to move from one discussion to another is to say to the group, "This was a useful discussion on the setting of this case. Now that you have a good sense of the community, let's look at some of the characters." The transition can be smoother, however, if you build on comments made by the participants: "Juanita, you noted that Martha Jones is pivotal for understanding this conflict. Let's look more closely at who she is and what her role might be."

Opening and Closing a Case

Use creative ways to begin and end the case discussion. For example, one leader opened a discussion of "Beyond the Battle" by asking the group to draw clues from the case to describe the city of Springfield. Another leader opened a discussion of "Prairie Storm" by asking the group to share words or phrases to describe their reactions to singing the national anthem. This revealed not only the diversity of the group but also the level of emotion that patriotism can evoke, a central issue in the case.

When concluding a case discussion, facilitators must resist the temptation to select the "best" alternatives or trump the group by suggesting that the facilitators know the best responses. Doing so poses dangers similar to those mediators face when they become arbitrators and assume responsibility for resolving a conflict. Parties can become disempowered and may not take responsibility for keeping decisions.

The most effective case discussions are frequently left open—they continue during the coffee break and even after the workshop. For example, one church group closed a heated discussion of the case "Lord of the Dance," involving a dispute between the deacons and a youth group, by listening to a recording and singing, "Lord of the Dance" (also known as "I Danced in the Morning"). Participants were energized by the singing and eager to begin the next section of the workshop.

Timing

The teaching notes that follow each case give approximate times for each section. It is important to plan the time you want to spend on each topic and keep close to your projections. However, a good case leader needs to be flexible and able to balance between a teaching plan and the participants' needs. This skill requires sensitivity and experience, but having a co-teacher who watches the time will help move discussions along.

Asking Good Questions and Promoting Dialogue

Good case teachers ask good questions and trust the group to do the hard analysis. When framing discussion questions, use open questions rather than closed questions. A closed question—for example, "What color is your new car?"—usually has one answer. An open question—"What are the most important factors in buying a new car?"—may have any number of responses. By using open-ended questions to stimulate dialogue, you are also modeling how to help disputing parties move from their declared positions toward sharing their underlying needs and interests—a critical skill in reaching a sustainable agreement. Asking people to elaborate on brief responses is another way to encourage dialogue. "Help me understand what you mean by that" leads to deeper analysis and can reveal unstated assumptions.

As your questions become more complex or probing, expect participants to disagree. Encourage them to discuss their differences openly: "Letitia, you indicated earlier that you felt that the corporate CEO focused only on the needs of his own business. Now Pablo is saying the CEO is concerned with the long-term welfare of the entire community. Talk to each other about this." As the case leader, you will be modeling how participants can disagree in a "safe" context.

After asking a question, do not be afraid of silence. Participants need time to consider their responses. Or you may need to rephrase a question for clarity. Filling the silence with your own response can rob the group of ownership of the discussion.

Using a Marker Board or Newsprint

Write an outline on newsprint or a marker board before discussing topics such as setting, contributing and causal factors, persons, alternatives, and resources. This provides a visual guide for the discussion. Space the topics according to how you want the newsprint or board to look at the end of the discussion.

Most case teachers strongly recommend visual recording or mapping of a discussion because it helps you do all of the following:

- Keep track of the discussion
- Show relationships between individual contributions and discussion topics
- Recognize and affirm the value of individual contributions and insights
- Help visual learners
- Provide a record of the full discussion
- Record specific topics for further use in the workshop
- Identify and analyze case characters to use in role-plays following case discussion
- Record goals and strategies developed in the case discussion for use in the role-plays

Use key words or phrases to record a discussion. When recording a complex insight, verify your understanding with the contributor. This models active listening, paraphrasing, and summarizing, which are primary skills taught in the workshop.

If you find that simultaneously leading and recording a discussion is too difficult, consider teaching the case with a co-trainer. Identify mutual goals, and discuss how you can work together to give participants equal access to the discussion. Co-trainers should feel free to enter the dialogue to check the intent or meaning before recording individual contributions.

Although many teachers use an overhead projector to record a discussion, most case leaders find them ineffective for encouraging group interaction and dialogue.

Size of a Case Discussion Group

You will often have to adjust your timing and goals to fit the size of a group. A group of ten to fifteen participants is more likely to engage in interpersonal dialogue and in-depth discussions than a group of forty or fifty.

Special Challenges

Many discussion leaders, particularly in large groups, often call on vocal people and unwittingly give the impression that these speakers' contributions are more valuable than those of quieter participants. Some people are naturally reserved and need the security of a small group to feel comfortable. If several participants are not speaking, consider dividing the plenary discussion into small groups and assigning them a specific question to discuss.

A serious issue in a multicultural setting is when cultural differences become an inhibiting factor. Numerous studies have shown that white people of Northern European descent unconsciously dominate in multicultural settings. A frustrating and even destructive power dynamic can develop in a group if this is not recognized and addressed.[2] A culturally sensitive facilitator can help counteract this tendency by being a good referee, taking care to balance contributions. An observant co-teacher can also help balance the discussion by looking for "quiet hands" or gentle signals from those who want to enter the discussion.

Summary

We have suggested several approaches for teaching case studies and identified benefits of using them. A case discussion provides a framework for workshop facilitators that serves many purposes:

- It encourages an elicitive teaching style.
- It models approaches for paraphrasing and clarifying issues.
- It models critical steps in community intervention.
- It challenges attitudes and stereotypes.
- It helps participants identify specific areas where they can apply peace-building skills.
- It offers a nonthreatening way to introduce difficult topics.
- It builds a sense of community among a group sharing a common experience.

In workshops that have a diversity of participants, a good discussion of the right case study offers additional benefits. These are particularly valuable for leaders who usually approach community conflicts as "lone rangers," often with disastrous results. An effective case discussion can heighten sensitivity to persons with different perspectives and increase appreciation for group analysis and conflict resolution from a variety of worldviews.

The intent of this chapter is to equip and encourage facilitators to dive in and lead a case discussion. If you are hesitant about case teaching, work with a partner. Also, consider asking a friend or colleague to observe your teaching style and privately share observations and concrete suggestions with you after the workshop.

Case teaching is not only fun but can also be extremely rewarding. A good discussion energizes a group, draws participants into a joint adventure, and sets the stage for a productive workshop.

ANNOTATED LIST OF CASE STUDIES, TEACHING NOTES, AND ROLE-PLAYS

Beyond the Battle

Martha Jones, a retired city schoolteacher and newly elected president of the Springfield Board of Education, prepares to chair her first board meeting. Her election platform was on building consensus in a historically divided board. Increased violence and weapons in the city schools led several school board members to propose installing metal detectors and adding security guards in affected schools. The only funds currently available in the school budget to support this action have been allocated for a package of long-term reforms initiated and widely supported by members of the public. The vote on the security measures is on the docket for this meeting.

Martha believes she holds the deciding vote, but she is seeking an alternative approach to the board pattern of win-lose decision making.

This case has been used effectively with groups of urban community leaders, many of whom have faced the same issues raised by the case. Workshop participants in six different U.S. cities have expressed the conviction that the case was written about their own community! Three progressive role-play scenarios introduce events that occur after the case events end and lead workshop participants through the stages of mediation. The third role-play involves a multiparty meeting.

Call to Prayer

A Muslim employee of a county social services agency declares that religious intolerance is at the heart of his being forced to move from his original office into a much smaller space. The agency director insists that the office is needed for the new department supervisor and suspects that the employee's disappointment in not getting the supervisor's job is at the heart of the complaint. Concerned that the dispute could affect other county departments and relationships with county clients, the director asks a trusted Muslim community leader to intervene.

This case raises the challenges of multicultural, multiracial, and interfaith communication. The single role-play is useful for practicing "getting parties to the table," as well as paraphrasing and distinguishing between positions and needs or interests. This is a good role-play for discussing the advantages and disadvantages of introducing a co-facilitator. It is easy to expand the role of the facilitator to that of a mediator and follow the basic steps of mediation.

Giving Thanks

Flyers were distributed by the Korean Merchants' Association to announce a local Thanksgiving Party and Turkey Giveaway to show appreciation to the predominantly African American South End residents for their business. These flyers were soon followed by unsigned flyers calling residents to join a protest march opposing the event and to "kick the Koreans out" of the neighborhood. Hoping to avert a serious confrontation, Korean Pastor Sam Lee meets with African American Pastor Joshua Taylor and several other South End residents to learn more about the situation. The Korean businessmen consider the information gathered by their pastor as they decide whether or not to cancel the party.

This case raises issues of cross-cultural communication, the power of stereotypes, and the role of trusted religious leaders in addressing community conflicts. It also raises the importance of having an awareness of the multiple layers of most community conflicts. The short case can be read quickly, and it challenges readers with both the destructive and constructive potential of interethnic conflicts. The first role-play focuses on paraphrasing and cross-cultural communication; the second involves problem solving. The third is a multiparty role-play.

Lord of the Dance

A congregational meeting erupts with an angry debate between supporters of the board of deacons, who defaced a specific hymn by marking it as "unworthy," and supporters of the youth group, which earned the money to purchase the new hymn books. Al Bannon, the moderator of the meeting, struggles to maintain order and devise a strategy to resolve the conflict. Bannon believes the conflict has deeper roots.

This case never fails to provoke a lively discussion. It provides a good opportunity for role reversal by urging participants who identify with the young people to empathically enter the perspective of the deacons, and vice versa. By adding parties previously identified in the case, the role-play can also be adapted easily to become a multiparty meeting.

SOURCES FOR ADDITIONAL CASE STUDIES

 The Jossey-Bass Web site, www.josseybass.com/peaceskills, contains several additional North American and international case studies, teaching notes, and role-plays designed specifically for use with this curriculum.

The Association for Case Teaching Case Clearing House includes more than nine hundred religious and social science case studies written by members of ACT. A significant number of these cases focus on conflict resolution. The ACT Case Clearing House is located at Yale University Divinity School, 409 Prospect Street, New Haven, CT 06511. An annotated case bibliography and order information can be obtained on the Yale Web site: http://www.yale.edu/divinity/case_teaching/. An annotated list of books containing case studies and commentaries, additional information on ACT, and a link to the ACT Case Clearing House is available at http://www.PlowsharesInstitute.com under the topic "Case Teaching."

CHAPTER 3

Encountering Sacred Texts

CONFLICT TRANSFORMATION workshops challenge peacebuilders to become advocates of a just process that restores relationships between adversaries and addresses unequal and unfair systems. What resources can motivate, sustain, and revitalize peacebuilders who become change agents and bridges between conflicting parties?

Colleagues from many cultures and faith traditions confirm that one source of energy and renewal is an encounter with authoritative, illuminating, and sometimes transforming texts. Serious engagement with a particular passage can convict the conscience, inspire the spirit, and even rejuvenate the body to pursue peacebuilding. Some texts may even appear to "read the reader" and open people to new insights that lead to personal transformation. Heinrich Zimmer (1993) speaks of such texts as "oracles of life." We have witnessed such encounters with sacred texts in many parts of the world. Alienated parties have been drawn together to pursue the struggle for understanding. Exhausted mediators have returned to the table with new commitment. Separated groups have discovered common ground in neglected resources.

Authoritative texts in this section of the Leaders' Guide are treated as "sacred" because they hold authority for specific religious traditions or a particular cause. Some texts are also considered "sacred" because they evoke religious commitment or elicit a sense of justice. The respect or revered nature of the text is rooted not only in its authority but also in its transformative power. For some participants, a text becomes authoritative because of its relationship to God, the divine, the transcendent, the holy. For others, a text has moral authority because of its meaning, profound insight, or historic importance in the journey of a community. Someone who does not believe in God may gain insight and wisdom from a sacred text or experience the text as transformative.

SPIRITUAL, MORAL, AND CULTURAL RESOURCES

Being a peacebuilder involves learning how to use special skills and techniques—analyzing conflicts, recognizing their destructive and creative potentials, and working cooperatively with others for the good of a whole community.

Being a peacebuilder is also a way of life. Peacebuilders and agents of reconciliation must be clear about their own assumptions and attitudes that can limit their openness to others. They must learn what blocks them from honoring—hearing, understanding, trusting, and learning from—an individual or group of people. Peacebuilders should also be aware of the source and understand the implications of the values that inform their actions.

Why is justice important? What does justice call for in this particular situation? These insights and abilities grow from one's spiritual and moral journey. They depend on one's being willing to seek self-understanding, to risk being vulnerable to change, and to continually seek the truth revealed in moral and spiritual resources. Peacebuilders also find in these resources the strength to continue working for peace in the midst of obstacles and even failure.

Shared reflection on sacred texts is one way to help community peacebuilders develop a greater understanding of the moral and ethical principles that shape their thoughts and motivate their actions. Prayerful or thoughtful personal application of shared reflections can be a powerful tool for increasing self-understanding and sustaining a commitment to the work of reconciliation.

Studying sacred texts can also help peacebuilders identify common ground or shared values between parties and communities, to bridge differences and build new relationships. Fresh, joint interpretation and application of sacred texts often provide additional support for a sustainable peace. For example, recovery of a common cultural value of hospitality, renewal of a constitutional promise of freedom, or recognizing a religious mandate for forgiveness may provide a breakthrough in negotiating a community agreement.

THE POWER OF ENGAGEMENT

The following examples illustrate the power of serious engagement with sacred texts.

> An Indonesian conflict transformation training program, Empowering for Reconciliation, is in its third year of equipping civic and religious leaders to respond to community conflicts that

are often rooted in cultural and religious animosity and misunderstanding. These workshops, which include participants from the Muslim, Catholic, Protestant, Hindu, and Buddhist traditions, provide opportunities for joint study of sacred texts that are chosen by participants. One workshop group selected passages from the Qur'an and the Confucian Book of Wisdom about forgiving your enemies and passages from the Christian New Testament on loving your enemies. A second study involved a role-play of the story of Jacob and Esau, which is an authoritative text for the "People of the Book"—Catholics, Jews, Protestants, and Muslims.

Participants at this workshop were inspired by the emphasis on forgiveness and reconciliation in these texts, but they were also deeply moved by the interreligious and intercultural dialogue the texts stirred. When evaluating the workshop, participants of different faiths noted that the most distinctive factors of the workshop were the transformation of relationships between group members and the recognition of how joint study of sacred texts can help in addressing conflict in their nation. The participants had expected to acquire skills to address conflict. They had not expected to change their perspectives or to build relationships across cultural lines or religious divisions.

• • •

The goal of a U.S. program was to enable trusted civic and religious leaders to transform their communities or congregations into centers of healing rather than sources of division. During one workshop, several Christian participants confessed that they often failed to follow the biblical mandate to be agents of reconciliation. Instead, they nurtured the forces of recrimination and division.

One pastor reached a personal turning point during an encounter with the New Testament parable traditionally known as the Good Samaritan. His group had reflected on the "woundedness" of the Samaritan traveler, an outcast from the dominant Jewish society who overcame his personal experiences of pain and discrimination to rescue a fellow traveler who had been assaulted and robbed. During the "application" section of the scripture study, the pastor drew a symbolic picture of his own wounds. He later shared that the scripture study was a major step in his liberation from dwelling on painful life experiences with racism. He made a personal commitment to use his experiences as a bridge to heal others and to stop using his anger as an excuse to avoid becoming a proactive peacebuilder.

Each time these oracles of life are consulted, they have the potential to uncover fresh insights. If individuals allow a passage to penetrate their protective assumptions, they can use its power to rearrange their perspectives about people and conflicts, which at first often seems overwhelming.

Interactions with texts from sources that are not defined as sacred or revered by the reader are also possible. Serious engagement with a bill of rights or scripture from a different religious tradition, for example, can have illuminating and empowering consequences. Often in a cross-cultural or interfaith workshop, individuals discussing how a passage affects them make a connection with life experiences of other people and feel a special bond in the quest for peace. Transformative insights occur with such frequency in different settings, cultures, and languages that they can even surprise workshop leaders who anticipate them.

APPROACHES TO STUDYING SACRED TEXTS

To draw illumination from an authoritative text, workshop leaders can take several approaches. We find one approach to be particularly helpful.[1] Walter Wink, professor of biblical interpretation at Auburn Theological Seminary in New York, has introduced this approach throughout the world in his books, courses, and workshops. Wink, who describes the methodology in *Transforming Bible Study* (1989), states that his personal quest as a biblical scholar was to find "a way to heal the split between the academic study of the Scriptures and the issues of life" (p. 17). With Wink's encouragement, persons and communities of diverse backgrounds and cultures have adapted this approach to their own context and applied it successfully to other types of authoritative and sacred texts.

Most of the guidelines for using case studies and role-plays in teaching apply to studying sacred texts: employing stories and problems for cooperative resolution, asking good questions, and trusting in participants' wisdom, experience, and insight. These are also valuable tools for empowering and equipping people to be effective peacebuilders. Asking open questions to identify the needs and interests that lie beneath one's initial demands is as important in studying authoritative passages as it is in using the mediation process. In the Christian New Testament, Jesus taught his disciples and challenged his adversaries by telling stories and asking good questions. The Jewish Talmud contains the insights of centuries of scholars who offer commentaries, tell stories, and ask questions as they discern how believers should apply the religious and ethical principles of the Hebrew code of law. Muslim judges apply the demands of the Qur'an to daily life.

Human beings participate in the power of religious texts through faith and shared beliefs. We, the authors, believe that God speaks to people in many ways—through sacred texts, God's action in history, and the witness of other believers—and engages them in ministries of reconciliation and justice. Although we come to the peacebuilding process through the Christian faith, we deeply respect the revered texts of other religious traditions, as well as the moral mandates that motivate individuals without a specific religious confession.

Following the guidelines for sacred text study is an annotated list of four sample texts. Authors who are rooted in the Judeo-Christian tradition developed sample questions for those texts in Chapter Nine that draw on Jewish and Christian scriptures. Authors from other religious and moral traditions selected and wrote questions for the other sacred texts. We refer to these as "sample" texts and questions because they are designed to encourage facilitators to develop their own questions for these and other religious, moral, and historic texts.

GUIDELINES FOR GROUP SACRED TEXT STUDY

The guidelines will assist workshop leaders in using the texts and sample questions.

The Leader's Preparation

1. Identify the themes on which you want the study session to focus. Select the text that best addresses these themes or concepts.

2. Carefully read the selected passage several times. Imagine the setting and the people involved in the story. Identify the sequence of events.

3. If you plan to use one of the texts with the prepared questions, first make a list of your own. Develop these questions in a logical sequence. Use the sample questions to supplement or enrich the questions you develop for your own group.

4. Although some information is included with the sample questions, look for additional background material on the text.

5. Save your last hour or so of preparation to center down and pray over your questions—for trust in them, in the process, and in the Spirit who makes everything come alive. Try praying for each person, if you know the group. Open yourself to creative happenings.

6. When you have prepared as thoroughly as possible, say to yourself, "I'm not certain how this text applies to this community. I come to it with the group as if seeing it for the first time, prepared to hear things I never knew or understood before."

Explanation of Dialogue Style

Some groups may be unfamiliar with this type of scripture study. To prepare those who feel they lack knowledge of sacred texts and might expect the leader to provide answers to all questions, make the following points:

> I will be asking several questions about the text. There are many possible responses to these questions, so don't think your answer is not good if I wait for more responses. Use periods of silence to reflect on the questions. In most cases, there are no right or wrong answers, so I won't approve or disapprove of your responses, except to correct any factual information that appears to be in error. All of us are experts at the level of our own experience.

> We are here to be open, to learn from each other. This method of approaching scripture affirms the presence of God or the Divine working through and among us. Come to the text with a fresh perspective, laying aside the remnants of preconceptions or old interpretations.

> It is important for everyone to take responsibility for participating in the discussion. We will be engaging in a conversation, so I will not expect you to raise your hand to speak. However, if anyone has difficulty entering the conversation, raise your hand to let me know.

Centering

Begin the sacred text study with a time of silence. A quiet pause helps participants put aside distractions and sharpen their senses. Ask people to get into a comfortable position, to close their eyes, to be aware of their breathing, to let go of tenseness or distractions, and to relax for a few moments. You can end the silence with a prayer involving an awareness of God's presence in the group and in the text.

Reading the Text

There are a variety of ways to introduce a primary text. Copies of the selected passage can be handed out. For many scripture studies, it is also helpful if each person has a copy of the full text. The leader can read the text aloud or ask various members of the group to read the text aloud one verse at a time. The study is more interesting if various participants read from texts in different translations and different languages.

An exception to this guideline is when the text is exceptionally long, and the goal is general understanding rather than careful study of the words. For example, sacred text study number two ("Healing and Reconciliation"), about Jacob and Esau, suggests that the leader tell rather than read the story, which covers nine chapters of scripture.

Overview: Discussion of the Text

Wink (1989, pp. 38ff.) notes three important elements in his approach to sacred texts:

1. Honor the text by approaching it in as open and fresh a way as possible. Most issues will surface through good questions. By studying commentaries on the text, the leader may add limited but important information no one present can provide. This use of critical scholarship helps protect the text from our blindness to personal assumptions and biases.

2. Amplification is the second element. Persons in the group discussion are asked to "live into the narrative" until it becomes real for them through imaginative exercises, role-plays, and mimes. People are challenged to understand and identify with one or more of the characters, seeking to discover the logic of the text. Continue to ask what meaning the images or metaphors have for the life of the one engaging the text. Readers can face the questions the text poses only if the text comes alive for them.

3. The last element is the application exercise. To grasp the text intellectually or to see contemporary parallels is not sufficient. The text needs to penetrate the reader's existence so that the social or personal questions with which one is struggling can be disclosed and perhaps healed and made new. Making a drawing, writing prayers or dialogues, engaging in movement, or small group sharing may unleash the text to confront one's heart and soul. The transforming power of encountering sacred texts comes most clearly in the application to life, and facilitators should persist even if participants are initially reluctant to enter this crucial phase. However, the application must not be a human relations gimmick. The leader must believe that revelatory exercises nourish and sustain the life of those who seek to be agents of reconciliation and transformation.

Leading the Study

1. When the session begins, trust that your questions have arisen from the text and can lead the group into the text. If silence follows your question, pause, and then repeat it. If silence continues, repeat or at most rephrase the question. Do not, under any conditions, answer it yourself, for participants will sense your self-doubt and mistrust of the questions and withdraw from your leadership. Give participants the time and inner space they need to hear the voice of the text and respond to it.

2. Be aware of where you are in your series of questions, but do not let that prevent you from attending fully to what people are saying.

3. Integrate important new questions that come from the group, but do not abandon your own questions.

4. If someone brings up a topic you plan to deal with later, you may decide to address it, or if it interrupts an issue inadequately discussed, ask the person to hold it and say that the group will come back to it. If you do delay consideration, always return to the question. Failing to do so is a blow to the person and to your credibility with the group.

5. If people debate with one another, encourage them to let their differences stand without trying to force a "correct" notion on anyone. However, errors in matters of fact should be matter-of-factly corrected.

6. When one or more persons dominate, involve others as tactfully as possible. You may say, for example, "We haven't heard from everyone," or "Let's give first chance to those who haven't yet spoken," and repeat the question. If you fail to limit those who dominate, the group's anger can undermine the whole process.

7. If you sense resistance in the group, it is best if you stop and ask people where they are. Volunteer your own perception, such as, "My reading of the group is . . ."

8. Above all, remember that this approach is not an end but a means. Look for God's action in the group as best you can. Be willing to be surprised. Do not, however, abdicate leadership to someone else or let the group drift. You are a facilitator of transformation, and your presence as a leader grants you an authority that the group will recognize.

9. If someone bursts into tears or cries silently and you believe the study material has evoked the feelings, be aware of it, but keeping a focus on the discussion will probably reduce that person's discomfort. If someone needs support, those sitting nearby may spontaneously provide it. If they do not, you may encourage them to do so or, as a last resort, stop and do so yourself. People generally will not break down unless they sense that the group is capable of supporting them. Overall, the expression of feelings is a good sign.

10. If things aren't going well and you feel yourself beginning to force things to happen, stop and internally relax your body, breathe deeply several times, and establish eye contact with whoever is speaking. By letting go of your need to control, you may be able to flow with the process better. If that does not seem to help, try guideline 7 on this list.

11. Plan your time backward, from the application to the central section to the introduction. Always make sure you have time for the application.

ANNOTATED LIST OF SACRED TEXTS

The following descriptions will help facilitators connect the texts with specific themes and portions of the curriculum. The text, sample questions, and application exercises are located in Chapter Nine.

Recognition and Listening

Mark 10:46–52 from the Christian New Testament concerns Jesus' encounter with a blind beggar, Bartimaeus. Study of the text reveals the power of recognizing every person's human dignity. Deep listening to another person's needs reminds people not to assume they already know what is needed. Being asked to declare needs enables people to accept responsibility for being healed. Themes of listening, paraphrasing, and conflict as opportunity for change emerge from this text.

Healing and Reconciliation

Genesis, chapters 25–32, in the Hebrew Scriptures and the Christian Old Testament records the encounter between two brothers in conflict. The text explores the process of family conflict and the journey that leads to reconciliation. This text is effective for introducing concepts of reconciliation, dealing with emotions, letting go of the past, and restoring relationships.

Forgiveness and Enemies

The Qur'an, chapter 60, verses 7–9, declares that Allah will create affection with those whom one considers enemies. Study of the text allows workshop participants to explore the meaning of forgiveness—dealing kindly and justly with enemies—and limits to affection for enemies. The themes of creating new relationships with former adversaries and reaching, monitoring, and adjusting agreements are enhanced by reflection on this passage.

Justice and Freedom

The Preamble to the Constitution of South Africa is a historic civic document that has assumed moral authority, not only for South Africans but for other citizens struggling to establish, sustain, or recover justice and freedom under democratic structures in their country or region. Shared reflections about this text enrich personal resources for mediation as well as promote themes of peacebuilding and reconciliation with justice.

SOURCES FOR ADDITIONAL SACRED TEXT SELECTIONS

Additional sacred texts, questions, and application exercises designed for this curriculum are on the Jossey-Bass Web site, www.josseybass.com/peaceskills.

Walter Wink's *Transforming Bible Study: A Leaders' Guide* (1989) also contains several relevant sets of biblical texts, questions, and application exercises.

Section Two

Workshop Designs

Chapter Four presents the design for the basic workshop on community conflict transformation. The average time it takes a facilitator to complete an exercise or a series of exercises in a particular section is noted in the detailed discussion accompanying the overviews (Exhibits 4.1 and 4.3). Time for the optional exercises is not included in the overall time for a section. A skilled facilitator should be able to manage a workshop with ten to twenty-five participants; a team of facilitators could manage a group of forty-five. Larger groups will frequently take more than the average time to complete an exercise.

The basic workshop was designed using a fourteen-hour, two-day intensive training format. Our experience indicates that this is the minimum amount of time required to provide an introductory exposure to mediation as a response to conflict. It is also the maximum amount of time many busy community leaders can dedicate to training.

The workshop design is flexible. The timing noted on the basic workshop sections is the amount of time necessary for *introducing* participants to the various concepts. For further skill development, the workshop can be expanded easily from two to five days by extending the times allotted for exercises and role-plays and including optional exercises in the basic design. Trainers can also integrate one or more sacred text studies and use the Application Exercises at the end of each chapter in the *Peace Skills* Manual. Those who use a sacred text to focus on a specific theme or use additional exercises to practice specific skills can also omit a session, such as the multiparty role-play, and still complete the basic workshop in fourteen hours.

Trainers can select portions of the basic workshop to use in specific settings or, to save time, omit optional segments that are helpful but not vital to the progression of the workshop. Some workshop leaders have found the material easily adaptable to business and professional settings. They report, for example, that a combination of "Approaches to Handling Conflict" from Section V, a discussion of "Approaches to Handling Conflict" with the exercise "Group Responses to Conflict" from Section VI, and training in paraphrasing can equip staff members to better handle personal and professional conflicts.

Throughout the basic design, you will find references to specific sections of the *Peace Skills* Manual. These are suggestions for group leaders only. The design of the workshop centers on participants' interacting with one another, not on reading large portions from the Manual during the workshop.

The workshop facilitator or leadership team must be very familiar with the material in the *Peace Skills* Manual to use the workshop design effectively. The best workshop leaders, however, are not bound by a text. They are knowledgeable about basic material and draw freely on their personal stories and culturally relevant illustrations to supplement their teaching. Trainers in the most effective programs identify and coach willing participants from one workshop to become part of the training team in future workshops.

Chapter Five presents designs for a three-hour to half-day introduction to mediation and a one-day introduction to mediation skills. Chapter Six contains design suggestions for advanced workshops for those who complete the basic workshop.

CHAPTER 4

Community Conflict Transformation Workshop
Basic Skills Training

Goal

To help participants develop personal and transformation skills and deepen their understanding of community diversity so that they may respond more effectively to conflicts.

Objectives

- To build relationships and a learning community among participants
- To enable participants to see conflict as an opportunity for transformation
- To introduce key concepts and skills of conflict transformation
- To provide an overview of the mediation process

DAY ONE

8:30 A.M.   Gathering/Continental Breakfast (optional but recommended)

9:00–10:40 A.M.   Sections I–VII

I. Introductions   **(15–20 minutes)**

A. Welcome by Sponsoring Organization

B. Introduction of Participants Ask participants to give their name and one expectation for the workshop. This allows people to identify themselves, assists the group with name pronunciations, and lets the leaders hear the range of expectations.

C. Introduction of the Leadership Team Give a statement (1–2 minutes) of why you are involved in the training.

EXHIBIT 4.1

Overview: Day One Agenda.

Time	Topic	Page
8:30 A.M.	Gathering/Continental Breakfast *(optional but recommended)*	
9:00–10:40 A.M.	Sections I–VII	
15–20 min.	I. Introductions	43
	A. Welcome by Sponsoring Organization	
	B. Introduction of Participants	
	C. Introduction of the Leadership Team	
10 min.	II. Background to the Workshop	45
5 min.	III. Workshop Goals and Content	45
20 min.	IV. Conflict in Our Lives	45
	A. Looking at Issues	
	B. Looking at Feelings: The Conflict Circle	
10 min.	V. Assumptions About Conflict and Learning About Conflict	47
	VI. Approaches to Handling Conflict	48
5–10 min.	A. Range of Approaches	
10 min.	B. Distinction Between Mediation and Arbitration	
(15 min.)	C. Group Responses to Conflict *(optional)*	
5 min.	VII. Introduction to the Case Study	52
10:40–11:00 A.M.	Coffee Break *(read or review case study)*	
11:00 A.M.–12:30 P.M.	VIII. Case Study Discussion	52
12:30–1:00 P.M.	Lunch Break	
1:00–1:10 P.M.	IX. Overview of *Peace Skills* Manual and Introduction to the Stages of Mediation	53
1:10–2:55 P.M.	X. Beginning the Process	53
30 min.	A. Paraphrasing	
20 min.	B. Before Mediation: Bringing Parties Together	
15 min.	C. The Introduction Stage: Providing Safety	
35–50 min.	D. Skills Application: Case Role-Play #1	
5 min.	E. Review of Learning and Identifying the Roles of a Mediator	
2:55–3:00 P.M.	Stand-Up Break	
3:00–4:15 P.M.	XI. The Storytelling Stage: Offering Understanding	60
15 min.	A. Introduction to Storytelling	
	B. Skills Application: Two Fishbowl Role-Plays *(optional)*	
(15 min.)	1. Encounter with TV News	
(15–30 min.)	2. Modeling the First Stages	
30–60 min.	C. Skills Application: Case Role-Play #2	
10 min.	D. Summary and Review of Learning	
4:15–4:30 P.M.	XII. Closing and Preview	64
4:30 P.M.	Leadership Team Meeting: Day One Analysis; Day Two Preparation	

II. Background to the Workshop   (10 minutes)

Objective

To clarify the context of the workshop *(Leaders: Study in advance the Introductions to the* Peace Skills *Manual and the Leaders' Guide.)*

Introduce, for example, the following topics:

- The development of workshops and their impact on community leaders in South Africa
- Basic guidelines for community conflict workshops
- The distinction between peacemaking and peacebuilding
- The concept of conflict transformation
- The necessary links between justice and peacebuilding
- The importance of training of diverse grassroots constituencies together
- A focus on nonprofessional peacebuilders

III. Workshop Goals and Content   (5 minutes)

Objective

To begin developing comfort levels and trust among participants.

 A. Prepare in advance, on newsprint or posters, the goal, objectives, and workshop components. Use the overall goals and objectives listed above, or adapt them to meet particular workshop needs. List workshop components such as "Introductions," "Attitudes and Assumptions About Conflict," "Conflict Analysis and Causes of Conflict" (case study), "Paraphrasing," "Distinguishing Demands from Interests and Needs," "Mediating Conflicts" (role-plays), and "Application to City or Community."

B. Review the workshop goals and content with participants to see if they match participants' expectations or need adjustment.

IV. Conflict in Our Lives   (20 minutes)

Objectives

- To help participants distinguish between rational analysis and personal feelings about conflict
- To demonstrate diverse reactions to conflict situations
- To promote relationship building

Prior to this exercise, explain that the facilitators will use a "nonviolent" method throughout the workshop to gain the group's attention.

Group facilitators will raise a hand to request the group's silence. Each participant should then stop speaking and join in by raising his or her hand. Emphasize that "a raised hand means a closed mouth." Practice the process. It will quickly and quietly refocus the group, particularly during small group discussions.

A. Looking at Issues Ask participants to think of a *specific conflict*—personal, professional, or community—in which they are or were involved. Ask them to think about the issues involved in the conflict and explain that they will be asked to share them with a partner. They do not have to use names or give specific details. Both will have less than five minutes to speak and will have to make sure that each has a turn. Make sure everyone has a partner before beginning. End the conversations in four to five minutes with raised hands.

This exercise leads to an energetic discussion involving everyone. It allows participants to share their personal understanding of conflict, and it clearly demonstrates the prevalence of conflict in everyone's life. If time allows, put three or four participants, rather than just two, in each group. When the groups are finished, work with the whole group in making a list of kinds of conflict that have been described.

B. Looking at Feelings: The Conflict Circle (*Leaders: Study "Responses to Conflict" in Chapter Two of the* Peace Skills *Manual.*)

1. Ask participants to get in touch with their feelings or emotions about the conflict they shared in pairs (or another conflict they feel strongly about).

2. Stand in the middle of the room and tell participants that you represent the conflict. Ask them to stand and position themselves in relation to the conflict, according to how they honestly feel, not how they think they should feel. Explain: "If you are very anxious and want to avoid this conflict, stand far away, but don't leave the room! If you feel like addressing this conflict immediately and directly, stand right in front of me."

3. After participants have positioned themselves, encourage them to share why they stood where they did. Those who stand "behind the conflict" may say they want to observe the conflict first and keep at a safe distance. Those who stand quite close or very far away might say they feel very angry or hurt.

4. Explain that this exercise is not intended to judge one's ability to deal with conflict or to help others deal with conflict. For example, some of the best facilitators and mediators are uncomfortable with conflict. However,

they have reflected on their reactions to it, sought to change unhelpful responses, and strengthened their skills and approaches to handling conflicts. Also, explain that where people stand in relation to conflict is affected not only by the specific conflict they identified but also by family and cultural patterns.

5. Before participants sit down, ask them to look around the room and observe the variety of positions and responses to conflict. If they are helping mediate or facilitate a dispute, they should remember that parties have very different emotional reactions to the same situation.

V. Assumptions About Conflict and Learning About Conflict (10 minutes)

Objective

- To identify underlying theoretical and educational assumptions that inform the workshop

(Leaders: Study Peace Skills *Manual, Chapter One, "Assumptions About Conflict," and Section One of the Leaders' Guide.)*

The following is one way you can share this important material with participants.

To focus the presentation, you may find it helpful to prepare in advance on newsprint or a poster a list of brief phrases or symbols for each category. Use personal stories and analogies to expand and illustrate the assumptions.

Assumptions About Conflict

- The Chinese characters representing crisis are formed by the symbols for danger and opportunity. Conflict involves both.
- Conflict can provide opportunities for change.
- Effectively addressing conflict is culture-specific. There is no one, "right" way to handle it.
- Peacebuilding is grounded in justice and human development.
- Conflict is normal and necessary, not a sign of failure.

Learning About Conflict

- The workshop provides time and space to reflect on and improve existing skills.
- The workshop is not for leaders to "teach" as much as it is an opportunity for participants to share ideas and learn from experiences.
- Growth in the workshop depends on a willingness to risk and make mistakes.

- The workshop should be a safe place where offering support and constructive feedback is the responsibility of both leaders and participants.

- Developing a covenant of confidentiality supports the goal of safety. (This is an agreement that all personal stories and reflections shared in the workshop would be considered confidential.)

VI. Approaches to Handling Conflict

Objectives

- To affirm the validity of many ways to deal with conflict, to locate independent outside intervention, and to compare the level of control that disputing parties have over the outcome *(Leaders: Study* Peace Skills *Manual, Chapter Two, "Understanding Conflict and the Role of Mediation.")*

- To clarify misconceptions about terminology and to focus on mediation skills *(Leaders: Study* Peace Skills *Manual, Chapter Three, "Mediation: A Tool for Empowering Others.")*

- To encourage reflection about attitudes toward conflict *within groups* and deepen understanding of the costs and benefits of different conflict management styles *(optional)*

 A. Range of Approaches (5–10 minutes) Refer to the *Peace Skills* Manual, Figure 2.1, "Approaches to Handling Conflict," or draw the diagram on a board or newsprint. Point out the range of approaches from negotiation to legislation, and explain that almost all may be appropriate at one time or another.

The diagram does not intend to imply that the step beyond legislation is violence. However, in many conflicts, when parties or group members no longer recognize the authority of the legal system or the government, they may regard rejection or overthrow of these structures as a viable option. Avoidance or violence can take place at any point in this diagram.

(If you draw the image on a board, introduce the approaches before adding the line indicating the "legal boundary" and the line indicating the degree of control parties have over their decisions. Circle or highlight *mediation* and *arbitration*. If you are working with a multicultural group, ask where distinctive cultural approaches to dealing with conflict fit into this range of approaches.)

B. Distinction Between Mediation and Arbitration (10 minutes)

1. Write the words *mediation* and *arbitration* on newsprint. Note that both approaches involve someone who is not party to the conflict in resolving differences.

2. Ask participants for their understanding of each term, distinguishing between the two approaches. List on the newsprint distinctive attributes of each.

3. It is important that participants understand the basic difference between these two approaches, namely, that an arbitrator decides what the solution will be and announces it to the parties, whereas a mediator merely facilitates or assists discussion between parties who make the decisions. The following diagrams may be helpful.

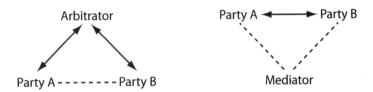

In arbitration the interaction is between the parties and the arbitrator. In mediation, the parties interact, supported by the mediator.

4. Acknowledge that there are appropriate times for using both mediation and arbitration.

5. Discuss why mediation might be particularly helpful for dealing with community disputes.

(If time allows, use section IV, titled Mediation and Arbitration Role-Plays, in the half-day mediation skills workshop portion of Chapter Five of this Leaders' Guide to reinforce understanding of the critical distinction between these two approaches—60 minutes.)

C. Group Responses to Conflict *(optional)*   (15 minutes)

Objectives

- To encourage reflection about attitudes toward conflict *within groups*
- To deepen understanding of the costs and benefits of different conflict management styles

Use this exercise to demonstrate conflict styles within two different community agencies.[1] You can easily modify it to discuss religious congregations or businesses. The discussion can be particularly helpful in settings where conflicts involve reactions to decision-making processes.

1. Draw the first seven letters of the alphabet in two circles. The letters represent staff members of two different nonprofit organizations. Identify each circle by name, or designate them Agency 1 and Agency 2 (see Figure 4.1).

FIGURE 4.1

Seven Persons at Two Different Agencies.

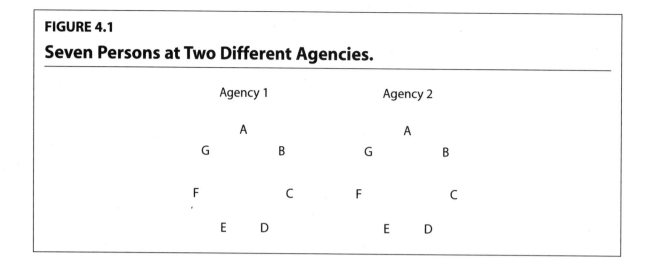

2. Agency 1 and Agency 2 face the same problems:

Funding—for staff and program support

Leadership—retaining the current director or "liberating" the director to pursue other professional options

Space—additional room for current and future staff

3. Explain that a wealthy organization has offered Agency 1 a substantial grant if staff members will shift their priorities and work on a special project. Persons A, B, and C want to accept the funds. Persons D, E, and F want to reject the offer, convinced it will compromise their standards. Person G is undecided. Circle the letters representing the different positions on the board. (Your drawing will now look like Figure 4.2.)

4. In addition, in Agency 1, Persons A, D, and G support retaining the current director. However, Persons B, C, E, and F feel it is time for the director to "share her skills with another organization." Draw two additional cir-

FIGURE 4.2

Lines of Conflict at Agency 1.

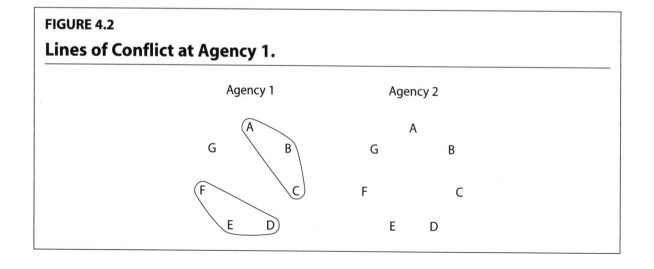

cles, preferably in a different color, grouping the positions. The circles will intersect.

5. Finally, staff members of Agency 1 are debating whether or not to move their offices into a larger building. Persons A, B, F, and G want to move into available space a few miles away, convinced that more space is urgently needed. Persons C, D, and E feel it is important for the organization to stay in the same place and remodel the office because the current location is closer to their clients. Draw the appropriate circles in a third color. The intersecting lines will make a "cross-stitch" pattern.

6. Amazingly, Agency 2 is having the same problems. Persons A, B, C, and D want to take the grant offered by the same wealthy funder with the same restrictions; Persons E, F, and G want to refuse the grant. The same people, A, B, C, and D, want to remove the director, while E, F, and G want to retain the director. Finally, A, B, C, and D want to move the office; E, F, and G want to stay in the same location. Draw the colored circles to group the positions for each conflict. Your two images will now look like Figure 4.3.

7. Whereas previous exercises have focused on individual responses to conflict, this one will draw out the advantages and disadvantages of ways in which groups deal with conflict. On your diagram, write "cross-stitched" under Agency 1 and "polarized" under Agency 2. These terms describe the effects of how the two organizations respond to conflict. Ask, "Which group would you prefer to work for and why?" Here are some additional questions you can ask:

- How do co-workers relate in the two organizations?

- How do power and win-lose decision making affect relationships?

- Which organization is probably afraid of conflict? What are signs of this?

FIGURE 4.3

Conflicts at the Two Agencies.

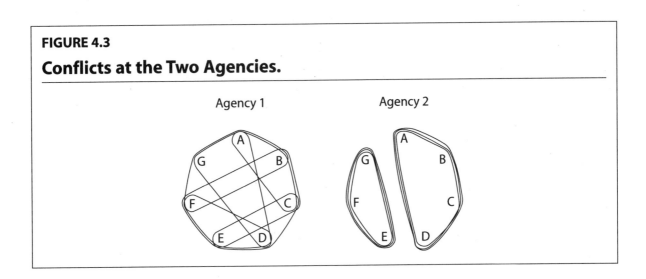

- Do you think the people in Agency 2 are divided by issues being debated or by other factors?

- Which organization may have unresolved conflicts?

- Which organization might actually be strengthened by conflicts? Why?

Here are some additional notes for this exercise.

- A healthy attitude toward conflict, as demonstrated by Agency 1, can strengthen an organization.[2] The majority of participants who discuss the differences between the two organizations usually affirms the benefits of working in an organization that encourages open discussion and offers opportunities for building a variety of coalitions. They are worried about an organization in which each additional issue further divides people who do not communicate well with one another. However, workshops will invariably include participants who feel more secure within polarized groups, and their voices need to be heard.

- To energize a large group, consider having participants stand in two circles as in the diagrams, connecting and raising their hands to represent the different positions described in the text. This takes longer but adds humor and action to the illustration. Have all parties return to their seats before the general discussion.

VII. Introduction to the Case Study   (5 minutes)
Objective

- To prepare participants for the case discussion (*Leaders: Study Chapter Two of this Leaders' Guide, "Case Studies in Conflict Transformation."*)

Select the most appropriate case study from Chapter Seven of this Leaders' Guide or the Jossey-Bass Web site, www.josseybass.com/peaceskills. Following the guidelines for presenting the case, in Chapter Two, introduce the selected case and explain the general objectives and direction of the case discussion. Use the handout "Problem-Posing Case Studies and How to Study Them" (Exhibit 2.1) to facilitate the discussion. Before beginning, be sure that all participants have read the case study.

10:40–11:00 A.M.   **Coffee Break**

Read or review the case study.

11:00 A.M.–   **VIII. Case Study Discussion**   (90 minutes)
12:30 P.M.

Objectives

- To help participants develop skills in four areas: analyzing elements of a conflict situation; understanding the demands (positions), needs, and interests of parties in conflict; developing strategies for intervention; and envisioning conflict as a resource for change

- To develop the background for the workshop role-plays

Carefully read your selected case. Study "Teaching the Case" and "Additional Suggestions for Effective Case Teaching" in Chapter Two of this Leaders' Guide, and follow or adapt the teaching note that accompanies the case you selected. Prepare in advance newsprint for the discussion outline and the RIVIRS analysis.

The central character of each case study is challenged by one or more immediate problems, and much of the discussion will focus on ways to address these problems. Consequently, it is important for the case facilitator to help participants envision the long-term goals of peacebuilding: empowering parties and communities to achieve reconciliation with justice. Keep these goals in mind during the case discussion and each role-play. Also, keep a clear newsprint record of the case discussion for ready reference later in the workshop, particularly of the characters or parties and group analysis of the sources of conflict.

12:30–1:00 P.M. **Lunch Break**

1:00–1:10 P.M. **IX. Overview of *Peace Skills* Manual and Introduction to the Stages of Mediation**

Describe the importance of the Manual as an interactive "home tutor." Note the Manual material already covered (Chapters One, Two, and Three). Then turn to the overview of premediation and the four-stage approach to mediation in Chapter Four, and briefly introduce the primary steps.

1:10–2:55 P.M. **X. Beginning the Process**

A. Paraphrasing (30 minutes)

Objective

- To raise awareness of the importance of active listening and practice a specific listening skill (*Leaders: Study* Peace Skills *Manual, Chapter Eleven, "Listening Skills."*)

1. Ask the group to identify skills and abilities a facilitator needs to move toward long-term, sustainable resolution of the case dispute (4–5 minutes). Make the question case-specific. For example, in "Beyond the Battle," what skills and abilities does Martha Jones need to help the school board reach a consensus as opposed to a win-lose vote on the proposal? In "Giving Thanks," what skills does Pastor Lee need to prevent a potentially violent confrontation?

Record key words and phrases on the board. (Responses may include *communication skills, listening, patience, trust, respect, understanding positions of different parties, analytical skills, ability to focus, collaboration.*)

2. Briefly introduce the importance of listening skills (3–4 minutes). Note that "active listening" or paraphrasing includes many of the concepts identified in the previous discussion.

- Ask participants how they know when someone is listening to them. List some responses on the board. Most responses will include *body language* such as *eye contact, nodding, leaning forward*. Note, however, that body language that conveys attention is culture-specific.

- In most cultures, communication is more than 80 percent body language and less than 20 percent words. You can demonstrate this by saying, "I really love you!" in a sarcastic voice and making exasperated hand gestures. Then ask the group the difference between the verbal message and what is communicated by body language.

3. Introduce the basic components of paraphrasing, which is one of the most effective ways to communicate listening and understanding. Post the following on newsprint.

Paraphrasing   Is repeating in your own words

Is focused on the other person

Is a summary

Is not parroting

Contains no judgment or evaluation

Acknowledges the emotional or feeling level of statements

Read and briefly amplify each point. Sensitive use of this form of active listening is one of the most important skills of a good facilitator.

4. Follow these steps for the paraphrasing exercise.

Develop a list of topics. Announce that participants will practice paraphrasing with a partner. Have the group assist you in developing a list of "hot topics" that offer polarized positions, such as abortion, capital punishment, corporal punishment of children, or legalization of marijuana. Be sure that the topics are clearly pro-con issues, not just social issues such as taxes or crime. Record the topics on newsprint.

Select a partner and a topic. Tell participants they will choose a partner and together select a topic about which the two disagree. They should choose their topic in a minute or two so that they have adequate time for the exercise. If they cannot find a topic on the list that they disagree on, they can choose another issue. Before the participants split into pairs, two members of the leadership team will demonstrate what each pair will be asked to do.

Demonstrate paraphrasing. Two co-trainers select one topic and sit facing each other in front of the group. The ground rule of the exercise is "You must paraphrase what your partner has said, to the satisfaction of your partner, before you respond." Person A makes a position statement about the selected topic, such as capital punishment. *(See the example in Exhibit 4.2. The demonstration team should begin with single, brief points.)* Person B then paraphrases A's position, gets an acknowledgment that it is accurate, and briefly responds to the point. Person A paraphrases B's response, gets acknowledgment, and offers a counterpoint. After three or four exchanges, stop the demonstration.

Practice paraphrasing. Instruct participants to choose a partner and begin their dialogue following this model. Ask participants to sit facing one another and start by making one, brief point at a time. If one does not paraphrase accurately, the dialogue partner should add to or correct the paraphrasing. Neither should use this as an excuse to make additional points. Allow time for each team to make eight to ten exchanges (8–10 minutes).

EXHIBIT 4.2

Paraphrasing About Capital Punishment: An Example.

A: I am absolutely convinced that capital punishment is wrong! There are too many times when someone convicted of a crime has later been proved innocent. Moreover, once someone has been killed by the state, it does not help much to say, "We're sorry."

B: One of the reasons you are strongly opposed to capital punishment is because legal decisions are not always correct, which is particularly difficult in decisions imposing the death penalty.

A: Right.

B: Well, I agree that the court system is not infallible, but this does not mean that the state should abandon imposing sentences on convicted criminals. We need a deterrent for murder, and the only appropriate sentence for one who has taken a life is to forfeit his own.

A: So you feel that the state should fit the punishment to the crime and that the death penalty is not only a responsible punishment but may deter others from committing murder.

B: Yes, that's my opinion.

A: But doesn't this mean that the state is justified in doing exactly what it says is wrong? I am concerned that the state models . . .

If necessary, post these directions.

- Identify a partner.
- Sit facing one another.
- Select a controversial "pro-con" topic about which you disagree.
- The ground rule is "You must repeat what your partner has said, to the satisfaction of your partner, before you respond."
- One party makes a brief statement about her or his position.
- The partner paraphrases the statement and checks if the paraphrase is correct.
- The partner responds to the point.
- The first party paraphrases this response, checks if it is correct, and responds, and so forth.

Guide participants. During the exercise, the leadership team moves quietly around the room and listens to the partners. Interrupt only if necessary to clarify instructions or assist a participant who is not listening well or does not understand the concept of paraphrasing.

Discuss the exercise. Regroup and ask participants what effects paraphrasing had on their communication. Summarize responses on newsprint. (Responses are likely to include *slows down argument, defuses emotion, forces parties to listen, helped me understand my own position better, not as far apart as we thought, moved beyond surface issues.*)

Ask group members if they have any concerns about the use of paraphrasing. Paraphrasing is not appropriate in all cultural settings, nor is it used in real life as intensively as in this exercise. Also, if the people doing the paraphrasing are not open and attentive, the technique can be manipulative and paternalistic. Ask participants for suggestions on paraphrasing effectively.

Summarize the benefits of paraphrasing. If paraphrasing is used appropriately and sensitively, it can be an effective way to communicate, not only by listening but also by understanding another person's perspective.

Explain that some participants will soon use paraphrasing in a role-play with conflicting parties who are not listening to one another. Two or more steps are necessary before they can begin the role-play. These steps involve getting the conflicting parties together in the first place and introducing the process of mediation.

B. Before Mediation: Bringing Parties Together (20 minutes)
Objective

- To identify responsible, culturally sensitive ways to encourage parties in conflict to meet (*Leaders: Read in advance Role-Play #1 for the case dis-*

cussed, and study "Getting the Parties to the Table" in Chapter Four of the Peace Skills *Manual.)*

1. Set the scene. Recall the strategies the participants suggested for constructive resolution of the case conflict. Ask them to adapt the following scenario to the specific case they discussed, using the update for role-play #1. For example, in "Giving Thanks," Pastor Lee and Rev. Taylor hope to arrange a facilitated meeting between two businessmen, Mr. Kennedy and Mr. Cho.

2. Conduct one or two brief role-plays. Ask one or two participants to become characters identified in the case. For example, in "Giving Thanks," Rev. Taylor or Pastor Lee might be speaking to Mr. Kennedy. The initiator's goal is to encourage the parties to agree to meet privately to discuss their differences.

3. Ask which approaches were most effective and why. What should the initiators avoid doing and why? What other aspects are important to include at this stage? Which aspects might be culture-specific? For example, in some cultures, an initiator would invite a trusted relative of the party to become a co-initiator. In some cultures, a telephone call is appropriate; in others, only a face-to-face meeting is acceptable.

4. Ask why the persons proposing a meeting might suggest facilitators or mediators other than themselves.

5. Advance the discussion by saying that the initiators were successful and both parties have agreed to meet to discuss their differences. Ask the group, "What is the best place for them to meet?" *(There are no "right" or "wrong" responses to this question.)* Have the group identify some guiding principles regarding choice of location.

C. The Introduction Stage: Providing Safety   (15 minutes)
Objective

- To enable participants to develop culturally appropriate ways to begin a session between conflicting parties *(Leaders: Study* Peace Skills Manual, *Chapter Five, "The Introduction Stage: Providing Safety.")*

1. Using the same case update (but now at the point of a facilitated meeting between the parties), ask, "What feelings might the two people have about the upcoming meeting?" Remind the group that the facilitator's limited goals for this meeting will be to provide an affirming, "safe" environment to help the parties better understand one another's concerns. Ask, "What are the most important things to do (in terms of room arrangement) and to say (in terms of greeting and process) to get the meeting off to a constructive start?"

2. List the suggestions on the board or newsprint. Highlight components that show appreciation toward the parties, help the parties feel safe (for example, guidelines such as not interrupting), state the goal for the meeting, and clarify the role of the facilitator.

3. *(optional)* If time allows, divide the group into pairs. Ask participants to spend a few minutes developing an outline of their opening statement. Each should then practice with a partner an introduction that is natural and comfortable (15–20 minutes).

4. Place three empty chairs in front of the group. Ask different people to come forward and arrange them for the meeting. Discuss what people feel are the most effective arrangements.

D. Skills Application: Case Role-Play #1   (35–50 minutes)
Objectives

- To practice creating a safe environment, assuring parties that the facilitator understands them
- To help parties listen to one another (*Leaders: Study Chapter One of this guide, "Using Role-Plays Effectively."*)

Explain that in the following role-play, the facilitator will be asked to use paraphrasing to promote understanding between two parties who are not paraphrasing. This is a central role of a peacemaker who mediates between conflicting parties. The facilitator wants to convey to the parties that even though they may not be hearing or understanding one another, they are still being heard and understood by the facilitator. The effects can be the same as those noted by the pairs in the paraphrasing exercise: slow down the argument, defuse emotion, and enable the parties to begin to listen to one another.

1. *Describe the role-play situation.* For example, in "Beyond the Battle" Role-Play #1, rather than facilitate the meeting herself, Martha Jones called on her friend Jorge Sanchez for assistance. In "Giving Thanks," Pastor Lee was asked by the parties to facilitate the meeting.

2. *Introduce the role-play.* Begin by discussing how to role-play as described in Chapter One. For example, say to the participants, "After carefully reading your role, turn the paper over and tape the name of your character on your shirt. Do not share the contents of your role with other players in your group. Stay in your role, and respond appropriately to the facilitator."

Remind participants of the general positions held by the parties identified in the case discussion. Explain that the purpose of the role-play is to practice introductions, paraphrasing, and brief summaries. It will last only ten to fifteen minutes, and there will not be time for the parties to make any decisions.

3. *Divide the group and hand out role-plays.* There are many ways to divide a large group for role-plays. If using the approach described in Chapter Two, ask participants to stand in three even columns (four columns if you use co-mediators). Assign roles by column. For example, those in the center are the facilitator, Pastor Lee; those on the right are Mr. Cho; and those on the left are Mr. Kennedy.

Suggest that each small group facilitator arrange the chairs. Begin the role-play after all announcements are made and teams are ready.

4. *Monitor small groups.* Members of the leadership team should select specific groups to monitor. Intervene only if necessary. Be sure each party gets to speak.

5. *Debrief in small groups.* Call "time" on the role-plays when the facilitator in each team has had sufficient time to introduce the session and each party has been paraphrased two or three times. Debrief the role-plays while participants are still in small groups. Ask the parties to state how they felt during the role-play. First, what did their facilitator do that was most helpful in enabling them to listen to one another? Second, what would they have done differently if they were the facilitator? Urge participants to be specific (5–10 minutes).

6. *Discuss what was learned.* Regroup for plenary discussion. Ask facilitators to share their feelings about their role. Discuss questions and record what participants learned from the role-play. (Topics might include *room arrangement, ways to provide "safety" for disputing parties, maintaining control, introductions, ground rules, laundering language.*) This is an excellent time to ask the group for suggestions about problems encountered and how they might best be addressed.

E. Review of Learning and Identifying the Roles of a Mediator   (5 minutes)

1. On a separate sheet of newsprint that can be saved during the workshop, begin to record notes on the goals and roles of a facilitator or mediator. (For example, aspects for this first role-play could be *provide safety, promote trust, offer understanding.*)

2. Refer participants to Chapters Five and Eleven in the *Peace Skills Manual.*

2:55–3:00 P.M.   Stand-Up Break

This is a good time for an "energizer" such as an active song or brief group game.

3:00–4:15 P.M. **XI. The Storytelling Stage: Offering Understanding** (75 minutes)

A. Introduction to Storytelling (15 minutes)

Objectives

- To show the potential of storytelling for building trust in the mediation process
- To demonstrate how a mediator can use storytelling to gather enough information to identify conflict issues and the parties' common concerns

An additional goal of this section is to highlight the importance of building relationships to sustain any eventual decisions about the conflict. A cornerstone of positive relationships between disputing parties is a mutual understanding of the needs and interests that influence the demands each party makes. *(Leaders: Review Chapters Six, Seven, Eleven, Twelve, and Thirteen in the* Peace Skills *Manual.)*

1. *Describe storytelling.*

- Parties on each side tell their story without interruption.
- Mediators paraphrase appropriately when needed.
- Mediators clarify details and identify interests through open questions or statements ("Tell me more about . . .").
- Mediators summarize each speaker's story.
- Mediators listen for common concerns and the central problems or issues.

2. *Raise the importance of "digging deeper."* The skill of helping parties move from the position they have taken in a dispute to discussing their real, underlying needs and interests is as important in storytelling as in the next stage, problem solving. To help clarify this point, draw a picture of a tree or bush that grows back from the roots when the top is cut off.

This bush regenerates like many conflicts when one addresses only the visible, "above ground" elements without dealing with the roots—the needs and interests that "feed" the demands. Often the conflict, like the bush, comes back even stronger when the symptoms rather than the causes are addressed.

3. *Discuss and demonstrate the skill of digging deeper or drawing out the parties.* (Refer especially to "Focus on Interests" in Chapter Seven in the *Peace Skills* Manual for further discussion of this important skill.) Remind participants that in the case discussion, they began to distinguish between demands or positions and the deeper interests of the case characters. Each character's role for the next role-play will contain more information than was disclosed in the case.

Ask: "If one of the goals of storytelling is to gather additional information, what are the best ways to do this if people are tense, angry, and defensive?"

After briefly sharing responses, have two trainers demonstrate the unhelpful effects of interrogating questions. (The strategy in this brief role-play is for the role-players to respond to each question with another demanding question, omitting references to "why" and effectively blocking the possibility of either party offering reasons.)

Use as a possible scenario a wife who has been waiting for her husband:

Wife: Who do you think you are coming in so late? Where have you been?

Husband: What are you doing waiting up for me? I'm not a child!

Wife: How can I sleep when you don't call me? Where were you?

Husband: Don't you trust me?

Ask what is happening. What are the effects of this type of question? (Possible responses are *makes people defensive, gives limited space for response, appears to assume guilt, seems like a trap, escalates the conflict.*) Point out that *what, who, how,* and *where* are terms of interrogation.

Ask for alternative approaches to the husband-and-wife scenario, such as asking genuinely "open" questions or making leading statements: "Help me understand . . . ," "Please say more about . . . ," "Describe . . . ," "Tell me . . ."

Ask the group to suggest statements that would change the dynamics of the previous role-play. For example, "I was worried about you. I don't understand why you didn't call." "I'm fine. We had a flat tire. Tell me why you were so worried."

Suggest that stating a desire for more information is usually more effective than asking a series of direct questions.

Note that another way to build understanding and trust in the mediation process is to highlight the primary concerns and interests of the parties in the mediator's summary of each person's "story."

4. *Introduce the storytelling role-play.* Use the same basic case update for the following fishbowl role-plays and the prepared Role-Play #2 for the full group. For example, in "Giving Thanks," Rev. Taylor has become concerned about the growing tension between factions among African Americans supporting either Eli Johnson's or Doris Allen's position on holding the block party. After Johnson and Allen confronted one another publicly about their differences, Rev. Taylor initiated a meeting between them to be facilitated by Juanita Gonzales.

- Write the parties' public demands on newsprint or the board.

- Remind participants of the demands, needs, and interests of the two parties noted in the case discussion. Both parties have accepted the initiator's suggestion that they meet informally with an outside mediator.

(If you omit the following optional role-plays, proceed directly to C. Skills Application.)

B. Skills Application: Two Fishbowl Role-Plays (optional) *(Including one or both of these role-plays depends on the leaders' goals and the amount of time available. A fishbowl role-play involves one group acting and all others observing. Do not give the parties a written text for the fishbowl role-plays. Choose and give advance briefing to two participants who appeared to understand the positions of the parties during the case discussion.)*

1. Encounter with TV News (15 minutes)

Objectives

- To introduce the role of the media in community disputes
- To illustrate the effects of a public forum, which can push parties deeper into their positions and away from resolution

Identify a local TV news reporter *(best played by one of the workshop leaders).* Describe the scene using the parties in Role-Play #2. Both parties are at a community meeting in the public library. They are leaving the meeting separately to meet with the mediator. As they leave the library, an aggressive local news reporter confronts them.

The "reporter" should have fun with this role. Use a paper cup for a microphone and be very pushy. Feel free to interrupt the parties, referring statements made by one to the other. The goal is to create tension and get a good argument going.

When the parties are sufficiently agitated, another workshop leader should be ready to call "cut" and ask the participants what is happening. (In all likelihood, the parties are becoming angry and defensive and hence further entrenched in their positions.) Ask the observers, Are the parties stating their needs? Interests? Why not? Discuss media roles.

Then explain that although public exposure can intensify a dispute, the media can also play an important, positive role in community conflicts. Discuss how parties in a community dispute might work positively with the press.

2. Modeling the First Stages (15–30 minutes)

Objective

- To help participants who are struggling with introductions, paraphrasing, or the general process

The facilitator in this fishbowl (*played by a leader or participant who seems comfortable with the process*) models an introduction and begins storytelling with a goal of moving the parties from hard, opposing positions, stated as demands, to greater understanding of one another. (*Do not give the written text to the parties.*)

Leaders should call "freeze frame" or "cut" once or twice to question the group about the facilitator. If the facilitator is succeeding, ask what the person is doing to assist greater understanding. If the facilitator is having difficulty, ask the parties or the group for suggestions. Focus on ways to elicit the parties' real interests and needs rather than continuing to restate their positions as they probably did when confronted by the reporter. If appropriate, raise issues such as questions, ground rules, or body language.

After the role-play, "derole" the fishbowl participants before asking them to return to their seats. Ask them how they felt in their roles. If they were wearing role-play name tags, have them leave these on the chairs in the center of the room.

C. Skills Application: Case Role-Play #2   (30–60 minutes)

Objective

- To practice storytelling by focusing on ways to help parties in conflict raise their real concerns and for facilitators to identify the problems or issues

(*If you omit the fishbowl role-plays, be sure to describe storytelling and cover the skill of digging deeper as well as the case update for Role-Play #2 before beginning this role-play.*)

Although the process is simple, a great deal of material is covered in the storytelling chapter. Rather than lecture in advance on aspects such as dealing with interruptions or taking notes, wait for the role-play debriefing to raise these issues. This is an excellent opportunity for the leader to assume the role of facilitator and recorder while redirecting questions to the group for insight.

1. Divide the group for a three-person role-play (four-person if you use co-mediators). Encourage those who have not played the role of the mediator to stand in the center column or columns. Hand out the roles. Leaders monitor the teams and assist as necessary.

2. Debrief in small groups before moving to the plenary discussion. Debriefing of this role-play offers opportunities to discuss issues such as the importance of ground rules, identifying issues, and phrases or approaches used by a mediator or facilitator to help parties share their concerns rather than restate their demands. If participants are having difficulty with reframing, laundering language, or highlighting the positive, refer them to the Application Exercises in the *Peace Skills* Manual, Chapter Twelve, or do these exercises in small groups during the workshop (*optional*, 20 minutes).

D. Summary and Review of Learning (10 minutes) Add to the list of the goals and roles of the mediator or facilitator. Refer participants to the relevant chapters in the *Peace Skills* Manual.

4:15–4:30 P.M.   **XII. Closing and Preview**   **(15 minutes)**

Give a quick summary of the day and a brief overview of the next day's schedule.

4:30 P.M.   **Leadership Team Meeting: Day One Analysis; Day Two Preparation**

The leadership team should meet briefly to analyze the day, identify concerns, and suggest ways to address them. Set up newsprint and arrange chairs for the next day. If you plan to use additional case-based role-plays, keep the newsprint of the case discussion in a central place.

DAY TWO

8:30 A.M.   **Gathering/Continental Breakfast (*optional but recommended*)**

9:00–9:20 A.M.   **XIII. Getting Started**

Objective

- To orient the group to the day and introduce co-mediation (*Leaders: Read "The Role of Co-Mediators" in the* Peace Skills *Manual, Chapter Four.*)

A. Welcome. Brief Review of Day One (5 minutes)

B. Overview of Day Two (5 minutes)

EXHIBIT 4.3

Overview: Day Two Agenda.

Time	Topic	Page
8:30 A.M.	Gathering/Continental Breakfast *(optional but recommended)*	
9:00–9:20 A.M.	XIII. Getting Started	64
5 min.	A. Welcome. Brief Review of Day One	
5 min.	B. Overview of Day Two	
10 min.	C. Introduction to Co-Mediation: Planning for the Role-Play	
9:20–11:00 A.M.	XIV. Introduction to Problem Solving and Agreements	66
15 min.	A. Lights On at the Retreat	
10 min.	B. One Approach to Problem Solving	
(10 min.)	C. The Incredible Paper Clip: Benefits of Brainstorming *(optional)*	
75 min.	D. Skills Application Role-Play: Neighborhood Conflict over Children and Dogs	
	Coffee Break *(incorporate into role-play)*	
11:00–11:20 A.M.	XV. Learning About Agreements	69
11:20 A.M.–12:20 P.M.	XVI. Personal Resources and Conflict History "Maps"	70
	A. Moral and Spiritual Resources	
	B. Maps of "Conflict History"	
	Alternative XVI. Building Cross-Cultural Understanding *(described in Chapter Six)*	72
	(Small groups conclude before or during lunch)	
12:20–1:00 P.M.	Lunch Break	
1:00–1:10 P.M.	Opening Session: Resources and Map Insights	
(1:10–2:50 P.M.)	XVII. Facilitating a Multiparty Meeting, Case Role-Play #3 *(optional)*	72
10 min.	A. Brief Review of the Stages of Mediation	
90 min.	B. Multiparty Facilitation Role-Play and Debriefing	
2:50–3:00 P.M.	Break	
3:00–3:15 P.M.	XVIII. The Power of Process	76
	A. Introduction	
(30–45 min.)	B. Process Stories *(optional)*	
	C. Thumb Exercise	
3:15–4:00 P.M.	XIX. Plenary Session: Relating Workshop Training to the Local Context	78
4:00–4:15 P.M.	XX. Evaluation and Closing Circle	79
4:15–4:30 P.M.	Leadership Team Debriefing	

C. Introduction to Co-Mediation: Planning for the Role-Play (10 minutes) *(This section can be introduced at any stage in the workshop, even before the first role-play on Day One.)*

Explain that the following role-play calls for a mediation team. Like previous role-plays, it involves diverse parties—in age, gender, and racial and ethnic identity.

1. Ask, "What are some advantages of having a team of co-mediators work with the parties?" "What are some disadvantages?"

2. Record group responses.

3. Discuss preparations that a mediation team can make to work together effectively.

9:20–11:00 A.M. **XIV. Introduction to Problem Solving and Agreements** **(100 minutes)**

(Leaders: Study Chapters Seven and Eight of the Peace Skills Manual.)

A. Lights On at the Retreat   (15 minutes)
Objective

• To engage the group in a basic approach to problem solving

Identify two people in the group; use their real names for this exercise. Suggest the following scenario. "Maria" and "Edith" arrive for a weekend retreat to find they have the last available room. They are friends who have been looking forward to the weekend and to spending more time together. However, as they prepare for bed, Maria learns that Edith must have a light *on* to go to sleep. Edith learns that Maria must have the light *off* to sleep.

Ask the group to identify Maria and Edith's common concerns *(staying together, common frustration, wanting to sleep, wanting to work out a solution)*.

Identify the issues in this conflict. (Possible answers might be *the light, one room, building their relationship, quality of sleep*.) Since Maria and Edith agree that this is the only room and that they want to stay together, they need to work out creative ways to address the situation.

Write *light* and *relationship* on the board or newsprint. Circle the word *light*, and have the full group brainstorm options for dealing with the light. Try to list at least ten options. (These might include *using an eye mask, leaving on the bathroom light, one sleeping in the bathroom, dividing the room with a blanket, using a flashlight*.)

Ask Maria and Edith to look at the list. Have each one select options that are not possible and cross them off the list. Continue until you identify the most acceptable options for both. Have the group recall the basic steps for resolving the problem *(identifying common concerns, identifying issues, creating multiple options, evaluating options, selecting final solution).* Point out that it is not always necessary to include every one of these steps in problem solving.

B. One Approach to Problem Solving (10 minutes)
Objective

- To suggest one of many approaches to problem solving

Explain that there are many ways to structure the Problem-Solving Stage. Summarize the following approach to problem solving on newsprint, and review it with the group. *(Refer to Chapter Seven of the* Peace Skills *Manual. The following outline expands the process used in "Lights On at the Retreat.")*

During the Storytelling Stage, the mediator has identified common concerns and issues. In the Problem-Solving Stage:

1. Point out the parties' common concerns.

2. Suggest the issues to the parties and get their agreement that these are the issues they want to discuss. List the issues in simple, impartial terms.

3. Select one issue at a time.

4. Use paraphrasing and summarizing to help the parties further clarify their interests, concerns, or needs related to the selected issue or problem.

5. Encourage the parties to generate several options to resolve the issue.

6. Ask the parties to evaluate possible solutions and agree on the best options.

C. The Incredible Paper Clip: Benefits of Brainstorming *(optional)* (10 minutes)
Objective

- To show the potential of brainstorming as one way to generate creative options

This humorous exercise is a good group energizer. It could also precede the "Lights On" exercise.

1. Post one or two sheets of newsprint, and ask for one or two volunteers who can write quickly. Hold up a paper clip. Ask the group to call out as many uses for the paper clip as possible. The volunteers will list the uses on newsprint.

2. Call time after one minute. Refer to the listed suggestions. Ask participants what they learned about brainstorming. Note how many possibilities the participants named because they did not stop to debate the suggestions. *(You can adapt this exercise to the local context. For example, a group in Los*

Angeles named twenty-five uses for an automobile; a Hong Kong group had thirty uses for chopsticks.)

3. Remind the mediators to recall the benefits of brainstorming as they look for options for the two neighbors in the following role-play.

4. Note that brainstorming is not effective if the parties are suspicious and tense.

D. Skills Application Role-Play: Neighborhood Conflict over Children and Dogs (75 minutes) *(Note: The profiles for this role-play are in Chapter Eight. A second role-play, "The Student and the Jazz Musician," also in that chapter, can be substituted for this section if it is more appropriate for your audience.*

You will be asking participants to apply all four stages of mediation in this role-play. The introduction and discussion of the Agreement Stage are intentionally omitted until after the role-play groups develop their agreements. It is also possible to introduce the Agreement Stage before the role-play.)

Objectives

- To practice the first three stages of mediation
- To give participants a sense of success
- To demonstrate a range of creative options

Provide instructions to the role-play groups:

1. Parties should get "into" their roles but respond genuinely to the efforts of the mediators.

2. Each group will have co-mediators.

3. Each group will try to reach a written agreement on one issue by the end of the allotted time.

Give newsprint and markers to each mediation team to record the issues they identify and the agreements reached on at least one issue.

After dividing participants into their roles and identifying the role-play groups, allow sufficient time for the co-mediators to meet and plan their approach. If the coffee break comes during this role-play, mediators can incorporate the break into their session by serving refreshments to the parties. The intensity of the role-play is heightened if those playing the parent and the elderly person (or the student and the jazz musician) also gather in their respective groups for a few minutes to discuss their role.

Give special attention to the debriefing. Emotions may run high in the role-play. Coaches can help break remaining tensions by asking parties to shake hands. In the plenary discussion:

1. Discuss general strengths and difficulties experienced by the groups.

2. Discuss the list of issues that the groups identified and how these were worded. The discussion will be more concrete if you post the issues identified by some groups. (This is also a good time to refer to the section titled "Clarify the Issues" in Chapter Seven of the *Peace Skills Manual*.)

3. Discuss the benefits and challenges of co-mediation. Ask for suggestions on how to address difficulties in the future. (*Usual problems include co-mediators not sitting together and uncertainty about how to communicate concerns or problems.*)

11:00–11:20 A.M. **XV. Learning About Agreements** **(20 minutes)**

Objective

- To identify principles for developing culturally sensitive agreements that can ultimately empower the parties to handle future issues more constructively (*Leaders: Read Chapter Nine in the* Peace Skills *Manual, "The Agreement Stage: Seeking Sustainability."*)

A. *Post the written agreements developed during the role-play.* (Focus on two or three.) Ask which agreements will probably work, which may not, and why. Develop a list of what the participants consider to be the most important elements of an agreement. Be alert to cultural differences.

(*Note to leaders: There are some basic principles that seem to apply in all cultural situations. These include clarity of who will do what, when and where; shared and balanced responsibility for addressing problems; and identification of a follow-up process. However, the specific form of the agreement should reflect the cultural norms of a given community. In some communities, a handshake is sufficient to seal an agreement, and insistence on a written document will be seen as an affront. In other communities, a written agreement is an important sign of commitment.*)

B. *Return to the lists of agreements.* Identify the agreements that stop at the immediate conflict and those that will foster a positive relationship between the parties. (*For example, are there any agreements that go beyond fixing the fence to inviting the elderly person to a meal or inviting the children to "meet" the dogs and play with them?*) Discuss ways the conflict between the two neighbors can be transformed, not only to build positive relationships but also to address any issues of injustice raised in the role-play situations.

C. *Review what has been learned about problem solving and agreements.* Add to the goals and roles of the mediator or facilitator, and refer to the relevant chapters in the *Peace Skills* Manual (5 minutes).

<table>
<tr><td>11:20 A.M.–
12:20 P.M.</td><td>**XVI. Personal Resources and Conflict History "Maps"**</td><td>**(60 minutes)**</td></tr>
</table>

(Allow small groups to decide whether to conclude their sharing before or during lunch. An alternative exercise, "Building Cross-Cultural Understanding," is noted below under Alternate Section XVI. These sections intentionally come before lunch to allow groups to extend their conversations. For many people, these are the most meaningful conversations in the workshop.)

Objectives

- To help participants identify their personal resources for dealing with conflict

- To help participants better understand the role conflict has played in their life

- To consider how their present responses to conflict are influenced by their "conflict history"

- To consider how their patterns of responses to conflict have changed over time

This opportunity for small group sharing can significantly deepen cross-cultural understanding. (*Leaders: Read Chapters Ten and Thirteen of the* Peace Skills *Manual.*)

Divide the group into teams of four. Check the composition of each team to balance gender, age, and ethnic or cultural diversity. (*The leadership team is encouraged to form its own group or to individually join a group of participants.*) Emphasize that participants will not be pressed to discuss anything they choose not to in their small group. Confirm their original agreement to a covenant of confidentiality about personal stories and issues that may emerge during the course of the personal sharing.

A. Moral and Spiritual Resources First ask the members of each group to spend a few minutes reflecting on their personal moral and spiritual resources for dealing with conflict situations. When they are in the midst of a painful conflict with someone, what keeps them going? When they become the bridge between two conflicting friends, family members, or colleagues, what personal resources enable them to continue in this often difficult role?

Then launch the exercise:

1. Suggest that people jot down their thoughts before briefly sharing them with one another.

2. Give small groups ten to fifteen minutes to share reflections with one another. Urge them to divide the time equally.

3. Call time. Explain that if some people have not finished sharing, they will have time in the next exercise to integrate and complete the sharing they began in their group. They may stay in their small groups for the following directions if all can hear and see the facilitator.

B. Maps of "Conflict History" *(It is possible to form different groups for the next exercise. However, experience indicates that the small groups have begun to bond and may be reluctant to begin with new partners.)*

The initial "conflict circle" and experiences in the role-plays showed the importance of a mediator's or facilitator's attitudes and feelings about conflict. How one feels about and responds to conflict have been shaped by a variety of experiences and values. Ask participants to think of their experiences with conflict as a "river" that winds through hills, descends into valleys, goes through rough places, and enters placid lakes. Along the way, they experienced many different conflicts and may have changed the ways they address them. Ask participants to reflect chronologically on conflicts that affected their life, recalling situations (such as their place in the family) or events that led to conflicts and how they responded to these conflicts. What in their "history of conflict" brought them to an intensive workshop on conflict transformation?

Have one large sheet of paper or a half sheet of newsprint and several magic markers or crayons available for each participant. *(A brief description of a "model" map drawn by a leader is usually helpful for participants.)*

1. Give participants ten to fifteen minutes to draw their own "map."

2. Encourage them to use symbols without any words and draw situations or events as accurately as they can.

3. Explain that the "map" is primarily for personal reflection.

4. Tell participants they will "decipher" their maps in the same groups of three or four. They will not be pressed to discuss anything they do not want to.

5. Write the steps for this exercise on newsprint:

   • Draw your own individual map.

   • Reconvene in your group.

   • Allot time for each person to discuss his or her map.

(Notify participants that lunch will be available at 12:20. Each group should feel free to adjourn when it has finished. Groups can continue sharing during lunch. The full group will reconvene at 1:00 P.M.)

11:20 A.M.– **12:20 P.M.**	**Alternate XVI. Building Cross-Cultural Understanding** **(60 minutes)**

(Small groups can decide whether to conclude their sharing before or during lunch.)

Objectives

- To explore how culture intersects with issues of conflict

- To discover ways mediators can reach across boundaries of personal and group identity

(Note to leaders: Because this exercise is equally effective in an advanced workshop, it is described more fully in Chapter Six of this Leaders' Guide, "Designing an Advanced Workshop.")

This exercise is most effective in multicultural settings. For groups who wish to focus on moral and spiritual resources, the session combines well with a one-hour discussion of Luke 10:25–37. This study can be found at the Jossey-Bass Web site, www.josseybass.com/peaceskills, under "Additional Sample Questions for Sacred Texts."

12:20–1:00 P.M.	**Lunch Break**
1:00–1:10 P.M.	**Opening Session: Resources and Map Insights**

Briefly process the resources and maps sessions (or sharing about cultural differences). Do not ask for personal information that the groups shared. Ask what people learned or found most helpful.

1:10–2:50 P.M.	**XVII. Facilitating a Multiparty Meeting; Case Role-Play #3** *(optional)* **(100 minutes)**

(Omit this section if you have extended the morning exercises into the afternoon or if you want more time for Section XIX, "Plenary Session: Relating Workshop Training to the Local Context.")

Objective

- To introduce some of the promises as well as the challenges of addressing a community conflict in a multiparty meeting.

Even if the participants had a sense of success in the dogs-and-children role-play, they will likely struggle with the difficulty of facilitating a multiparty meeting in this role-play. It is not realistic to assume that any real conflicts will be resolved in the time available, but participants will be able to heighten their sensitivities and practice their growing skills in a safe environment. Although it is late in the day, the role-play is energizing and should be introduced with enthusiasm.

A. Brief Review of the Stages of Mediation (10 minutes) *(Also refer to the role of the mediator or facilitator developed during the workshop.)* Lead this review session as elicitively as possible, drawing on the participants' memory of the stages of mediation.

B. Multiparty Facilitation Role-Play and Debriefing (90 minutes) *(This is an eight-person fishbowl role-play. "Beyond the Battle" and "Giving Thanks," in Chapter Seven of this book, and "Chaos in Carlton," on the Jossey-Bass Web site, have scripted multiparty role-plays. Role-Plays #1 or #2 for other case studies can be expanded for this session.)*
Use the following approach to conduct the multiparty role-play.

1. Introduction Before beginning, point out that there will not be enough time in this role-play to reach final agreements. As in real-life, some or all of the parties in the multiparty role-plays represent a group or an organization and do not have authority to make agreements without the consent of a wider constituency. Mediators will have to be alert to the need—often overlooked by parties themselves—for wider consultation before finalizing agreements.

2. Case Update Present the case update that precedes each multiparty role-play. Write the names of the parties and their specific demands or positions on the board or newsprint. State that the two meeting facilitators, agreed on by all parties, have done a great deal of advance preparation. They have contacted the parties and gotten agreement on some basic ground rules, including the agreement that one person from each team will make a brief, two-minute introductory statement.

3. Plenary Discussion of Facilitators' Role (15 minutes) Before dividing into roles, have all members of the full group consider themselves the facilitators. Ask what they want to accomplish in their opening comments. What kinds of ground rules should they suggest? How should they state their roles as facilitators? What is their strategy for facilitation? How should they arrange the room?

4. Forming and Preparing Teams (15 minutes) Have an equal number of participants choose one of the four roles, forming three teams of parties and one team of facilitators. Each team will meet separately to "get into" the respective roles. Facilitators will need the most preparation time. Therefore, select them first and release them to a separate room with one trainer to discuss their role.

Each group is to discuss its role and select two representatives for the role-play. For example, a workshop of forty will separate into four groups of ten. The ten who assume the role of the school board will meet and select the school board representatives, "Martha Jones" and "Thomas Jackson."

If possible, a leadership team member should meet with each small group to help participants clarify their positions and feelings, identify their needs and interests based on the role-play script, and discuss where they may be willing to make compromises. Each group then selects its two representatives and decides which one will speak for the team. All in the group help develop the representatives' two-minute opening statement.

5. Setup When the teams are ready, the two selected facilitators should arrange eight chairs in the middle of the room with all other participants sitting outside the circle. Those watching the fishbowl should be warned that they will be "silent observers" until a member of the leadership team calls for a "freeze frame" in the meeting. (No cheering or booing the teams!) Role-play facilitators should have an easel, markers, and notepads readily available. *(Leaders: Supply name tags for all fishbowl representatives, and urge them to have fun with this role-play!)*

6. Role-Play During the fishbowl role-play, the leadership team selects optimum moments for "freeze frames" (breaks) to ask observers how things are going, what is going well, and what they might do differently if they were the facilitators. Use "freeze frames" and suggestions when appropriate to glean important learning points for the facilitators, the fishbowl parties, and the observers.

Continue the role-play thirty to forty minutes. If there is more time, the learning may be more substantive.

After completing the Introduction Stage and the initial statements in the Storytelling Stage, some trainers find it helpful to "fast-forward" the process. They move ahead, for example, to identify common concerns and issues for five to ten minutes, then select one issue for discussion, and so forth. This approach offers an overview of a process that could realistically take from several hours to several days or weeks.

7. "Deroling" (10–15 minutes) Being part of a fishbowl role-play in a large group can be stressful. Therefore, allow sufficient time to "derole" the players. First ask how each person felt during the role-play. Identify what the facilitators did that was helpful and what the parties might have changed if they were the facilitator. Also, allow time for the co-facilitators, who risked the most, to offer their evaluations. Other techniques to relieve tension after the role-play include asking the role-players to shake hands or having participants leave their name tags on the chairs and sit with the other participants. Subsequent plenary discussion and analysis can then be more objective and valuable for all participants.

8. Plenary Discussion (30 minutes) This type of community meeting is challenging to facilitate. However, if managed well, a meeting of community leaders can lead to greater understanding, reveal unexpected common ground, and become a constructive component of community conflict transformation.

Use the following questions to help facilitate the plenary discussion:

- What did you learn about multiparty facilitation?
- What was most important for good communication?
- What blocked the parties?
- What future steps could be taken to address the "causal and contributing factors" that surfaced during the case analysis?
- Reflecting on the Day One case discussion, reevaluate the original goals and strategies developed by participants in light of the progress made in the three role-plays. Discuss how some of these goals could be implemented.

2:50–3:00 P.M.   **Break**

3:00–3:15 P.M.   **The "Hand Tangle"**   **(10–15 minutes)**

The following section, the Power of Process, uses a brief activity to energize the group. If you omit this section, consider the following activity, which fits here as well as in other sections of the workshop, particularly following a role-play. (Note: This activity can be physically demanding and is not appropriate for many persons with physical handicaps.)

Form circles of seven to nine people each. Tell people to stretch out their hands toward the center of the circle, move forward, and each person take a hand of two different people. They may not hold the hand of the person standing next to them. Pause to check that all groups are accurately "connected." Then tell each group to work slowly and carefully to "unwind" and form a single circle without letting go of one another's hands. It is all right to turn backward or even have crossed arms in the finished circle. Some groups may end up with two separate circles, and some may not be able to succeed. The facilitators or a member of a group that has completed its circle may assist groups still working to unwind.

While still standing, process the exercise, asking how each group accomplished forming its circle. (Responses may include "We all needed to change position," "We used outside assistance," "We had to cooperate," and so forth.) Compare these responses to those needed to begin resolving a conflict. Especially if you have an "unsuccessful circle," remind the group that some conflicts cannot be settled by negotiation or mediation.

XVIII. The Power of Process   **(15 minutes for A and C;**
60 minutes if including B)

Objective

- To demonstrate the importance of process and the impact one's assumptions have on a process

(Leaders: Read "Designing a Peacebuilding Process" in Chapter Fourteen of the Peace Skills *Manual.)*

A. Introduction Refocus on the case discussion and role-plays.

Decisions made about a particular conflict are important. However, there are many instances when the processes used to reach those decisions have a greater and longer-lasting impact than final decisions or outcomes. Tie this notion to the case study, the *Peace Skills* Manual illustration of making coffee, or a personal story. In the case study on dogs and children, for example, the way the mediating neighbor handles the situation with the boys' parent and elderly dog owner may be more important than the specific details of the agreement. Peacebuilding is often as much about the process used to address differences as about the specific resolutions.

B. Process Stories *(optional)* **(30–45 minutes)** This exercise is helpful for a group focusing on community conflicts. It is also effective in an advanced workshop. If time is short, it may be omitted.

1. In plenary session or small groups, ask people to share a story of when they experienced a situation where they or others were upset not because of an outcome but because of a bad process.

2. Identify several principles for designing a good process, particularly in a community conflict. *("Designing a Peacebuilding Process" offers several illustrations.)* Consolidate what is learned and reaffirm that peacebuilders must take responsibility for designing a good process.

C. Thumb Exercise

Objective

- To illustrate that the *assumptions* peacebuilders bring to a situation will directly affect the kind of processes they design

This exercise is fun and energizing and never fails to get everyone involved. Because many participants will make false assumptions about the exercise, some will be upset with the "messenger" unless you give precise directions.

1. Ask everyone to stand and face a partner.

2. Tell the teams you will be demonstrating a "thumb exercise." Say explicitly that "the object of the exercise is for each person to get as many points as possible." *(Do not say "thumb game"; that could imply winners and losers.)*

3. With another trainer, hold up your right hands, locking the fingers of your right hands together with your thumbs touching.

4. While demonstrating, explain that to get one point, you must press down your partner's thumb. Your partner gets a point by pressing down your thumb.

5. State that each team will have exactly thirty seconds.

6. State, emphatically, two very important rules:

   • Partners may not talk to one another.

   • Partners may not hurt one another.

7. Without further discussion or questions, say, "Ready, set, go," and begin timing. Most teams will struggle trying to get one or two points per person, assuming that they must compete with one another for points. Usually, however, at least one team will begin to cooperate and quickly get twenty-five to thirty points each in the allotted time. If you do not see anyone doing this, a team of leaders who know the exercise can get the points.

8. Call "stop." Ask those who got at least two points to raise their hand. *(Several will probably have this many.)* Then ask for five, ten, or more. Ask those who scored high to share their "secret" with the group. Although the leader never states that the exercise is competitive, those who make this assumption will not get as many points as those who assume that the exercise can be cooperative.

9. Close this session with a reminder of the importance of the assumptions we all bring to the processes we design and employ to deal with conflicts. Mediators who assume that people are not capable of making their own decisions soon move to arbitration. When interveners assume they have the right answers or best approach to a conflict situation, they may find their excellent suggestions rejected because their process was not acceptable.

3:15–4:00 P.M. **XIX. Plenary Session: Relating Workshop Training to the Local Context**
(45–60 minutes)

(Leaders: Read Chapter Fourteen of the Peace Skills *Manual. Additional material on addressing community conflicts can be found on the Jossey-Bass Web site. Either workshop leaders or local hosts and coordinators can lead this session. The session frequently identifies areas of need and leads to concrete next steps and personal commitments by participants to address specific issues.)*

Objectives

- To help participants relate the training to their community
- To help participants take ownership for addressing their concerns and applying their skills as community peacebuilders

Ask participants to identify specific issues or areas of conflict their community is facing where proactive peacebuilding could make a difference and where *they* could play a role.

Identify and post four to eight local issues.

Divide participants into small groups of their choice, with each group focused on one of the issues. There may not be a group for all of the issues raised.

Give clear instructions to the small groups and post on newsprint:

Small Group Goals

- Share concerns about the issue or situation that you chose.
- Respond to the following questions:

  Who are the primary parties?

  What are possible strategies for intervention?

  For this conflict to become an opportunity for transformation, what can I do personally? (be specific)

  What resources can I (or we) draw on?

- Summarize primary group decisions on newsprint.
- Write your name on the newsprint.

Note that some workshop groups use the local application time to discuss the role of voluntary peacebuilders in their communities. They also take steps to plan additional workshops by identifying those who could benefit from similar training and participants who could assist as coaches in future workshops.

4:00–4:15 P.M.   **XX. Evaluation and Closing Circle**   **(15 minutes)**

Objective

- To conclude the workshop by affirming the participants and raising an awareness of mutual support

Broaden the discussion of things learned to the entire content of the workshop. One way to do this is to review the workshop goals. Ask, "What new skills or ideas came from the workshop?" "Are there ways you see conflict differently now?"

Form a closing circle of the entire group. Ask participants to cite one learning, insight or skill they may be able to apply immediately or one that will help them pursue peacebuilding in their community. Avoid "going around the circle." Instead, let those who would like to speak do so. Close with appreciation for the participants' commitment and serious investment in the workshop.

Ask participants to complete a workshop evaluation before they leave. Useful questions include the following:

- If we were to do this workshop again, what components should we be sure to include?

- What changes would you make?

- How will you apply what you have learned in this workshop?

4:15–4:30 P.M.   **Leadership Team Debriefing**

CHAPTER 5

Designs for Brief Introductory Workshops

My colleague and I would like to develop mediation skills for our work in the neighborhood, but we need a wider group to make the training most effective. How can we convince other community leaders that this program is a worthy investment of their time?

Members of our citywide Leadership Program have all expressed an interest in a course in basic conflict skills, but they can only give a day for introductory training.

Is there some way our staff members could have a short demonstration workshop to energize them for a full two- or three-day commitment?

THE FOLLOWING two workshop designs offer alternatives to respond to these concerns. Although a minimum of two to three days is needed for most people to become acquainted with basic mediation skills and approaches, there are times when it is not possible to meet this goal.

Both the half-day and one-day workshops draw components from the basic workshop design presented in Chapter Four. However, they also include different exercises or case studies to encourage participants in an introductory workshop to enter a longer training session. We refer to the short courses as a "tasty appetizer to whet the appetite for a solid meal."

Rather than provide the full *Peace Skills* Manual, facilitators of introductory sessions can assemble a small packet of material for participants. This can include sections such as "Assumptions About Conflict," "Understanding Conflict," "Mediation: A Tool for Empowering Others," "Listening Skills, "A Four-Stage Approach to Mediation," and, for the one-day workshop, the case study and the handout "Problem-Posing Case Studies and How to Study Them" (Exhibit 2.1 in this Leaders' Guide). Many participants will request copies of the full *Peace Skills* Manual or receive it when they take the longer course.

The same principles of elicitive training and a focus on conflict transformation are as integral to the brief workshops as they are to the sessions described in the basic workshop.

HALF-DAY MEDIATION SKILLS WORKSHOP (3 TO 4 HOURS)

Sections in this design are fully described in Chapter Four. Plan for a break between Sections III and IV or IV and V, depending on the components you choose.

Objectives

- To enable participants to see conflict as a resource for transformation
- To highlight the distinction between arbitration and mediation
- To introduce paraphrasing as an important skill for addressing conflict
- To encourage participants to attend a full training session

I. Introductions   (35–40 minutes)

A. Introduction of the Hosts and Leadership Team (10 minutes)

B. Introduction of Participants (5–10 minutes) Ask participants to share in the plenary circle their name and one distinguishing factor, such as their role and responsibility in an organization or an interesting personal fact.

C. Explanation of Process Explain the "nonviolent" process for calling the group together.

D. Introduction to Conflict *(Basic Workshop, Section IV)*

1. Ask participants to think about a specific conflict they know about or one they are involved in.

2. Divide the group into pairs.

3. Ask pairs to share the primary issues of the conflict, not the names of the persons involved. *Conversations will become quite animated.* (10 minutes)

4. Use the nonviolent process to call people back to the plenary discussion.

E. Types of Conflict *(optional)* Quietly listen as pairs are sharing. Identify one person who has a clear grasp of the issues and is willing to share more about the conflict with the full group. When the pairs return to the plenary session, ask the person selected to share with the full group.

As the participant describes the conflict, ask the group to help identify the causal or contributing factors according to the suggested "types of conflict." (Peace Skills *Manual, Chapter Two, "Understanding Conflict and the Role of Mediation," and Leaders' Guide, Chapter Two, the RIVIRS diagram, Figure 2.1).* Record the conflict types as they are raised, or suggest the types of conflict first and ask the group to match the issues with them (15 minutes).

F. Closing If you have used segment E, close the session by summarizing the importance of understanding the nature of conflict and how understanding conflict can help address it.

If you have omitted segment E, close the introductory session by noting the group's strong common experience with conflict.

II. Workshop Goals and General Schedule   **(5 minutes)**
List these on newsprint and discuss briefly.

**III. Conflict Circle, Assumptions About Conflict, and Learning
About Conflict**   **(20–30 minutes)**
Follow the basic workshop design (Sections IV and V), but select the most relevant material for the group's context and specific goals.

IV. Mediation and Arbitration Role-Plays   **(60 minutes)**
(Leaders: Study Peace Skills *Manual, Chapters One and Two, and Leaders' Guide, Chapter Four, Session VI B. Alternative Section IV below offers a fifteen- to twenty-minute approach to this topic.)*

Objectives

• To help participants clarify the difference between mediation and arbitration

• To gain a better understanding of the role and value of mediation

• To develop self-awareness in those who unknowingly tend to arbitrate rather than mediate

• To establish an environment of participatory learning

Because there are many steps in this exercise and people can get confused, it is unrealistic for a leader to give complete instructions at the beginning and expect the group to follow them without assistance. Step by step instructions work better.

A. Role-Play #1 (15–20 minutes)
1. Begin by asking the group to explain the difference between mediation and arbitration. List on newsprint a few key words offered by the

group to characterize each approach. Explain that in the role-plays that follow, the group will first experience the use of arbitration and then mediation. To prevent confusion, write on the board:

Role-Play #1: Peacemaker ARBITRATES.

Role-Play #2: Peacemaker MEDIATES.

It is important that the group understands the basic difference between arbitration and mediation. An arbitrator decides what the solution will be and announces it to the parties. A mediator facilitates or assists discussion between parties who make the decisions themselves.

2. Form groups of three for the role-plays. *(Both role-plays for this exercise are in Chapter Eight. Do not duplicate copies of the prepared role for the Concerned Neighbor in either role-play.)* Have each group identify one person to be Neighbor East, a student; another as Neighbor West, a jazz musician; and one to be a Concerned Neighbor, who plays a peacemaking role.

3. Have each party read his or her own brief from the role-play "The Student and the Jazz Musician." Instruct the parties to read only their own role. Remind those who are the Concerned Neighbor that in this role-play they are *arbitrating*, not mediating. They will not get a written script. It is their job to listen to both parties, make a decision, and tell the parties what to do. *(You may also brief people for their roles orally in another room, meeting for a few minutes with those who are the student, then with those who are the musician.)*

4. Begin the role-play after participants have a few minutes to read their roles and clarify questions about the exercise. The role-play will last fifteen minutes.

After ten minutes, announce that there are five minutes remaining for the role-play. Urge the Concerned Neighbors to decide now, if they have not already done so, what the solution will be and to announce this solution to the parties. End the role-play when the fifteen minutes are up.

B. Role-Play #2   (15–20 minutes)

1. Without discussing the first role-play, give assignments for the second role-play, "Neighborhood Conflict: Children and Dogs." People should stay with the same role-play group.

2. Explain that this is another neighborhood; there is no relationship to the first conflict situation. In this role-play, the Concerned Neighbor is again in the role of peacemaker but now serves as a *mediator* and should carefully avoid telling the parties what to do. Neighbor East, an elderly person, and Neighbor West, a parent, should read their roles. The groups will not have time to complete the mediation, but they have sufficient time to get a "hands-on" feeling of what mediation is like.

3. After you call time at the end of the role-play, ask participants to shake hands to help them get out of their roles. Have each small group stay together to discuss the following question: "Which approach, mediation or arbitration, did you prefer, and why?" (10 minutes).

4. Bring everyone back into the large group, and invite people to share their conclusions. *(If time is short, you can omit the small group discussion and go directly to the plenary discussion.)* Make a list of the strengths and weaknesses of both arbitration and mediation. You will find that in many small groups, the parties prefer the mediation process, while many facilitators prefer arbitration. Discuss why. Also discuss why mediation might be important for community conflicts.

Alternative IV. Distinguishing Between Mediation and Arbitration
(15–20 minutes)

Objective

- To clarify the difference between mediation and arbitration

- To highlight the effects of different approaches to conflict in a community context

1. Put on newsprint or make photocopies of "Responses to Conflict" from Chapter Two of the *Peace Skills* Manual.

2. Briefly identify and discuss each response category. Ask why parties lose an increasing amount of ownership and control of the process as they move toward the right and cross the "legal boundary."

3. Discuss the strengths and weaknesses of mediation and arbitration. Record key insights and summarize.

V. Developing the Skill of Paraphrasing   (45–60 minutes)
Objective

- To practice paraphrasing, a valuable communications tool for peacemakers *(Leaders: Read* Peace Skills *Manual, Chapter Eleven, "Listening Skills.")*

Follow the guidelines for Section X.A, "Paraphrasing," in the basic workshop.

VI. Evaluation and Closing   (15–30 minutes)
A. Tailor the closing session to reflect your specific workshop goals. For example, ask:

- In what kinds of situations could you use paraphrasing?
- What new insights or ideas did you get during the brief seminar?
- Are there specific areas (in your organization or community) where mediation approaches to conflict resolution may be useful?
- What kinds of additional training would your organization or group be interested in receiving?

B. In a closing circle, ask participants to cite one new point or insight they can apply now.

ONE-DAY WORKSHOP: INTRODUCTION TO MEDIATION (7 TO 8 HOURS)

Most sections of this design are fully described in the basic workshop presented in Chapter Four.

Advance Preparations

Choose the most relevant case for the group from Section III of Chapter Seven or the Jossey-Bass Web site, www.josseybass.com/peaceskills. Have copies of the case study and the handout "Problem-Posing Case Studies and How to Study Them" (Exhibit 2.1 in this Leaders' Guide) available for each participant, even if you mailed these out for advance reading. Also consider having available a brief set of selected pages from the *Peace Skills* Manual. These might include selected passages from Chapters One, Two, Three, and Eleven.

It is not always necessary to have a booklet of handouts for a group, but some "take-home" material is very helpful, especially in a brief workshop. As a minimum, in addition to the case study and the case handout, provide copies of Exhibit 3.1 from the *Peace Skills* Manual, "The Stages of Mediation."

Objectives

- To enable participants to see conflict as a resource for change
- To introduce key concepts and skills of mediation (for example, conflict analysis, paraphrasing, distinguishing demands or positions from interests and needs)
- To lay the groundwork for additional training

8:30 A.M.   Gathering and Light Breakfast

9:00–10:40 A.M.   Sections I–VI

I. Introductions

A. Introductions by the Hosts   (5–10 minutes)

B. Introduction of the Group   (5–10 minutes)
If people in the group know one another, ask participants to write down three single words that describe themselves. Then ask them to give their name and share the three words with the group. In more formal settings, ask people to state their name and their professional role.

C. Introduction of the Leadership Team   Give a brief explanation of why you are involved in the training.

II. Workshop Concepts, Goals, and Schedule   (5 minutes)

A. List on newsprint and briefly describe the distinctive components of the workshop: the importance of drawing on the skills and experience participants already have, active interchanges with others, an emphasis on long-term peacebuilding, and so forth.

B. Identify clear, simple goals.

C. Provide a brief sketch of events on newsprint. This could include "Assumptions About Conflict," "Conflict Analysis (Case Study)," "Paraphrasing," and role-plays.

III. Conflict Circle, Assumptions About Conflict, and Learning About Conflict   (30 minutes)

Follow the basic workshop design (Sections IV and V), but select the most relevant material for the specific group's goals and context.

IV. Group Responses to Conflict *(optional but relevant for many groups)* (15–20 minutes)

Follow the basic workshop (Section VI.C.), contrasting styles of dealing with conflict in two organizations.

V. Definitions   (10 minutes)

Briefly distinguish between negotiation, mediation, and arbitration, using insights from the group. State that the focus of the workshop will be on mediation, an approach with which most people have little experience.

VI. Case Study Introduction   (5 minutes)

Introduce the case study, and encourage participants to use the break period to read or review the case.

10:40–11:00 A.M.   **Extended Coffee Break**

Use this time to read or review the case study.

11:00 A.M.– 12:15 P.M.   **VII. Case Study**   (75 minutes)

A. Analyze the case situation. Refer to the basic workshop, Section VIII.

B. Build the identities of selected case characters, emphasizing the distinctions between their demands or positions and their interests and needs.

C. Focus primarily on the case characters in the first two role-plays.

D. Save time to work on creative alternatives.

12:15–1:00 P.M.   **Lunch Break**

1:00–1:10 P.M.   **VIII.** *Peace Skills* **Manual Introduction**   **(10 minutes)**

Introduce selected pages from the *Peace Skills* Manual from which you have already drawn. *(See the note on advance preparations at the top of this agenda.)*

If you did not prepare a booklet of materials, go directly to "The Stages of Mediation" (Exhibit 3.1 in the Manual). Copy this from the Manual or outline it on newsprint. Explain that during the afternoon, participants will use several basic mediation skills and approaches. Role-plays will introduce them to the first two stages, Introduction and Storytelling, which will prepare participants for the final two stages, Problem Solving and Agreements.

Rather than focusing intensely on the stages of mediation, this one-day design highlights specific skills for providing safety and understanding for parties in conflict. The leader should use the material in the basic workshop selectively; drawing on what is useful and omitting material that is too complex for this introductory session.

1:10–1:45 P.M.   **IX. Paraphrasing**   **(35 minutes)**

A. Introduction Follow the guidelines in the basic workshop, Section X.A., "Paraphrasing." Identify with the group the skills and abilities the primary case character or peacemaker will need to help bring short- and long-term resolution to issues in the case. (These might include *communication, listening, patience, objectivity, trust of parties, respect for parties, ability to draw on parties for expertise and information.*) Use this list of skills and abilities to describe paraphrasing.

B. Hot Topics Develop a list of "hot topics," demonstrate paraphrasing, and conduct the paraphrasing exercise in teams of two.

1:45–2:30 P.M.   **X. Paraphrasing: Role-Play #1**   **(45 minutes)**

Follow the guidelines in the basic workshop, Sections X.C. and X.D.

2:30–3:45 P.M.   **XI. Distinguishing Demands from Interests and Needs**   **(75 minutes)**
Objective

- To learn how to encourage people to move beyond their demands or positions and be willing to share their interests and needs.

Shape this section using selected material from the basic workshop (Section XI.A., "Introduction to Storytelling") and "Focus on Interests" in Chapter Seven of the *Peace Skills* Manual.

A. Review the difference between demands (positions), interests, and needs as discussed in the case (5 minutes).

B. Discuss the effects of different kinds of questions and different ways to gain greater understanding of parties in conflict (5 minutes).

C. Role-Play #2 Follow the basic workshop, Section XI.C., "Skills Application: Case Role-Play #2." If you have sufficient time, include the fishbowl role-play in Section XI.B.1., "Encounter with TV News."

Begin the exercise by offering a case update and writing the parties' public demands on newsprint or on the board. Be sure to leave sufficient time to debrief the role-play in small and plenary groups.

Conclude by discussing what people learned about the distinction between public positions and demands and actual needs and interests. Do not focus on the more detailed material in the basic workshop debriefing section.

XII. The Power of Process *(optional)* (15 minutes)

Use the Introduction to the Power of Process and the "Thumb Exercise" (Sections XVIII.A. and C. in the basic workshop) to stress the importance of attending to process in long-term peacebuilding.

3:45–4:30 P.M.   XIII. Evaluation and Closing

Follow the guidelines for the basic workshop (Section XIX). The time you will need for this section will depend on the nature and goals of the group and the goals of the hosts. During the closing plenary session, ask the participants to reflect on and discuss the events of the entire day. For example, ask, "What new insights or ideas did you get that relate to your professional or personal life? To the life of the group?"

Form a closing circle and share the learning, insights, and new skills people can begin to apply immediately (10 minutes).

CHAPTER 6

Designing an Advanced Workshop

AN ADVANCED WORKSHOP is as important for building a strong network of community leaders who can address local conflicts as basic workshops are for increasing the number of people trained.

An advanced workshop is also a follow-up session that may occur two to six months after basic training. Advanced workshops are often attended by 30 to 75 percent of the participants from an original training session. They provide an opportunity to those who received basic training to share how they are using their skills and to develop new ones. Unlike the basic workshop, which does not focus on local conflicts, an advanced workshop is an ideal setting for discussing and gaining support for addressing specific community issues.

Workshop leaders can adapt the following suggestions to half-day and full-day advanced sessions. Although some components are appropriate for any advanced workshop, leaders should keep in mind that the advanced workshop should be tailored to the identified needs of the group. Mediators with local experience are uniquely qualified to lead or assist with the advanced sessions.

(Be sure to have name tags available. Even participants representing the same constituency may not remember colleagues' names from one workshop to the next.)

I. Catching Up   (30–60 minutes)

Objectives

- To share personal experiences of using basic mediation and facilitation skills

- To further develop a support network for community peacebuilding
- To provide group assistance and insight for analyzing and addressing specific situations

A. Write on the board or newsprint:

How have you used skills or concepts from the basic workshop?

What have been your primary challenges?

B. The challenges of peacebuilding:

1. Renew a covenant of confidentiality within the group for the following discussion.

2. Request that persons involved in conflicts discussed not be identified by name.

3. Ask participants to share briefly (2–3 minutes) how they have used things they learned from the basic workshop. Remind them of skills such as paraphrasing, distinguishing demands and positions from needs and interests, and objective analysis of a situation. Ask whether they applied their skills in their home, business, congregation, or community.

C. Identify the challenges or problems people encountered in specific situations. *(If you were not able to canvass participants in advance, use this discussion to identify their needs and concerns to shape the workshop agenda.)*

D. Use the following exercise to form a base for addressing some of the issues that participants raised as challenges or problems.

1. Identify in advance one or two people who are willing to share briefly a specific conflict situation in which they have been involved. Ask them to identify what happened, the issues or problems involved in the conflict, the parties involved, and the causes of the conflict.

2. Involve the group in assisting with further analysis of the conflict. If it has not been resolved, discuss possible intervention steps the participant could take or should have taken.

II. Analysis of a Community Conflict (1–2 hours)

Use this approach if the situation is a community conflict that all or most of the participants are familiar with.

Objectives

- To analyze objectively a community conflict in a group discussion
- To make room for the expression of differing interpretations

- To identify central problems and generate creative options for addressing them

See "Designing a Peacebuilding Process" on the Jossey-Bass Web site, www.josseybass.com/peaceskills, for concrete suggestions.

A. Draw on newsprint or hand out copies of the visual image of a conflict shown in Figure 6.1.

B. Discuss the specific conflict based on this image. Use newsprint to record key words and phrases of the discussion. As a facilitator, you will need the skills of a good mediator, that is, being alert to the possibility of very different perceptions of the situation and taking care not to favor the interpretation of one party over others.

1. Begin the discussion by building the history of the conflict as known by the people present. The history can be one of the most revealing aspects of an analysis by a diverse group; significant events cited by some parties may be unknown by others (10–15 minutes).

2. Identify the primary parties or people, the social setting, and the issues or central problems (10–15 minutes).

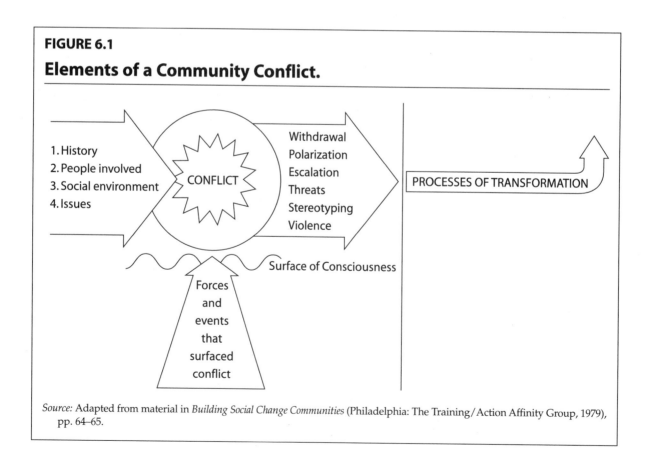

FIGURE 6.1

Elements of a Community Conflict.

Source: Adapted from material in *Building Social Change Communities* (Philadelphia: The Training/Action Affinity Group, 1979), pp. 64–65.

In discussing the social setting, consider changing demographics and political and economic factors. To what extent are group or individual identity issues, stereotypes, or prejudices identifiable elements? (There may be strong differences of opinion among the group. Remind participants that as in their earlier case analysis, people see the situation from their own worldview; a realistic picture is composed of many facets.)

3. Continue to fill out the "picture" of the conflict, mapping the event or events that surfaced the conflict; then identify the range of reactions and feelings experienced by the people identified earlier (10–15 minutes).

4. As you move to address the conflict, have people identify both short-term and long-term goals. Also consider what kinds of responses would escalate the conflict and what responses would deescalate the tension (10 minutes).

C. In plenary or small groups, work together to develop specific strategies to meet these goals.

1. If you formed small groups, ask each to write on newsprint its specific goal or goals and three to five concrete steps or strategies.

2. Post the newsprint, and have participants move around and read the suggestions silently.

3. Use the final fifteen to thirty minutes to build group consensus on appropriate, concrete steps that members of the group could take.

III. Building Cross-Cultural Understanding (60–90 minutes)

Schedule this session one hour before lunch so that small groups can conclude their sharing before or during lunch.[1] If time is limited, omit Step 5.

This session is most effective in multicultural settings. For groups wishing to focus on moral and spiritual resources, the session combines well with a one-hour discussion of Luke 10: 25–37 (see the Jossey-Bass Web site, www.josseybass.com/peaceskills).

Objectives

- To deepen understanding of cultural, ethnic, and racial differences in conflict situations

- To discover ways to reach across the boundaries of personal and group identity

- To explore sensitive and appropriate ways mediators and peacebuilders can respond in cross-cultural situations

A. Personal Insights Write the following phrases on newsprint. Ask participants to write a brief response to each and then to share their responses with the group. *(Do not record responses.)*

One aspect of my culture I'd like to change is . . .

What I would like to change in relating to multicultural groups is . . .

B. Looking at "Cultures" Cultural differences in a conflict can intensify emotions and influence commitment to a position. Some conflicts are based on cultural differences. Others have different roots but are complicated by culture. To be effective, mediators need to understand their own cultural identity and be sensitive to how cultural frameworks affect parties in conflict.

Step 1

1. Ask participants to define "culture." (Responses may include *values, beliefs, norms of behavior, ethnic identity, factors that shape our perspectives.*)

2. List the definitions on the board or on newsprint. (You may want to add your own definitions or others, such as *"Within your own culture it is what everybody knows that everybody else knows."*)

3. Ask the group to name some different cultures. List these on the board or on newsprint. (Responses may include *race, ethnicity, gender, class, age, education, geography.*)

4. Explain that intercultural conflicts can involve any of these factors. Each person in the room is in all of these categories. All of these cultures shape belief systems and assumptions about appropriate responses or reactions. People often hold these beliefs and assumptions more firmly when they are being challenged.

5. Draw an iceberg on the board or on newsprint.

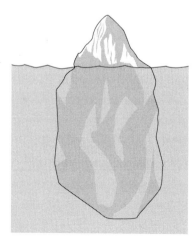

Explain that culture is much like this picture. People see what is "above the water"—skin color, what people eat, how people speak. However, these are only on the surface. The effects of someone's cultures go much deeper than surface observations can reveal.

Step 2

Tell the group that what people write in the next exercise is for their personal use. They will not be asked to share the details. Hand out pens and a sheet of paper, and ask people to fold the paper in half.

1. Ask participants to list on the left side of the page the assumptions others have about them because of their "cultures." (Allow five minutes.)

2. Have them list on the right side things that these stereotypes mask or hide about them, such as their gifts, abilities, skills, and perspectives. (Allow five minutes.)

3. Ask the participants to compare the two lists. Think about the following questions and then discuss them in plenary session, one at a time:

   - What is your response to the stereotypes people hold about you? (*Feel misjudged, frustrated, lonely, struggle to explain myself,* and so forth)

   - What are the personal and social effects of these assumptions and reactions? (*Protectionist laws, people overlooked, dehumanization, people shaped by images,* and so forth)

   - Who does the image making? (All of us!—different forms and types of media, parents, and ourselves)

Step 3

1. Identify in advance and list on the board or on newsprint eight distinct "identities." You might use case study characters from the basic workshop, for example:

Korean American deli shop owner	African American schoolteacher
White suburban homemaker	Latino jazz musician
University environmentalist	Black preacher
Asian student	Corporate CEO

2. Ask participants to turn their paper over and fold it to make eight boxes. Put one of the eight identities in each box. Without censoring their thoughts, they should write down a word associated with each identity. (*Participants will not be asked to show the paper to anyone else.*)

3. Allow five to ten minutes for participants to record their word associations. Then ask the following questions, leaving time for personal reflection.

- Look at the list. With whom do you feel the most sympathy? Affinity? *(Do not discuss.)*

- Who is the hardest for you to understand? *(Do not discuss.)*

- Where do these feelings come from? Ask for verbal responses from the group. (These may include *experience, lack of experience, media.*)

Step 4

1. Form diverse small groups of four. Write the following questions on the board or on newsprint, and ask the groups to discuss them. *(Allow at least twenty minutes for the small group discussions.)*

- How might the cultural images you hold of others or images others hold about you influence your role and overall effectiveness as a mediator or peacebuilder?

- How might your responses to these images affect a mediation situation?

- What can you as peacebuilders do about this?

2. Gather as a full group. Ask the group to choose someone who has not responded much in plenary to report on the group's discussion. Record the responses. List the "what can you do" responses separately. Go over the responses. Stress the importance of self-awareness and of people understanding their own images and stereotypes, the danger of cultural generalizations, and the role co-mediators and the mediation process play in effective, unbiased mediation.

Step 5

Ask each participant to choose as a partner someone in the room who is likely to come from a different cultural background. Explain that you will give all participants a paper with questions about how they react to certain situations. Hand out photocopies of Exhibit 6.1, "Some Cultural Differences That Affect Conflict Transformation." Participants are to read and respond to the questions themselves. They will then join their partner to compare and contrast their responses. Pairs should take the time remaining before lunch (approximately fifteen to twenty minutes) and as much of the lunch

EXHIBIT 6.1

Some Cultural Differences That Affect Conflict Transformation.

Check the response that feels most natural to you.

Getting to the point
- ☐ Don't beat around the bush; quickly identify and discuss the issues in a conflict.
- ☐ It is rude to name problems too quickly; it is better to spend some time in casual interaction first.

Saving face
- ☐ Admitting that you have been wrong, or backing down, is unpleasant but appropriate in some circumstances.
- ☐ Losing face is completely unacceptable.

Attribution of fault
- ☐ Defending oneself against an accusation is a sign of innocence; silence signals guilt.
- ☐ When people are defensive when accused, it shows they are guilty; to ignore an accusation is a sign of innocence.

Function of argument
- ☐ Heated argument escalates conflict and interferes with finding solutions.
- ☐ Heated argument is part of the truth-seeking process and helps resolve conflict.

Active listening
- ☐ Nodding and saying "mm-hmm" means "I am paying attention to you."
- ☐ Nodding and saying "mm-hmm" means "I agree with what you are saying."

Being silent while others discuss
- ☐ Silence is neutral; it simply means someone is not ready to speak.
- ☐ Silence represents agreement with what is being said.
- ☐ Not speaking when others exchange views is a refusal to help resolve the conflict and is obstructive.

Eye contact
- ☐ It is natural and respectful to look directly at the person you are talking with. Looking away may signify evasion or deception.
- ☐ It is natural and respectful to look away while talking with someone. Direct gaze may signify challenge or attack.

Questions
- ☐ Questions indicate interest and genuine concern.
- ☐ Questions are a form of attack; it is intrusive to require people to explain themselves.

(Continued)

EXHIBIT 6.1 (Continued)

Some Cultural Differences That Affect Conflict Transformation.

Issues and Questions for Discussion:

1. How do you and your partner differ in your responses to these situations? To what do you attribute these differences?

2. What are the implications of these differences for mediation and peacebuilding in cross-cultural situations?

3. How do your own moral and spiritual resources help you deal with cultural differences?

Peace Skills Leaders' Guide by Alice Frazer Evans and Robert A. Evans with Ronald S. Kraybill. Copyright © 2001 by Jossey-Bass Publishers, San Francisco.

Source: Based on material developed by Chel Avery of the Friends Conflict Resolution Programs, Philadelphia, and appearing in the third edition of the *Mediation and Facilitation Training Manual: Foundations and Skills for Constructive Conflict Transformation,* edited by Ron Mock (Akron, Pa.: Mennonite Conciliation Service, 1995), pp. 142–143. Used with permission.

---

period as they desire to finish their conversations. Caution people to be careful not to build stereotypes from what they learn in this discussion. The responses of their partner will be determined by a variety of factors and may or may not be unique to that person.

You can also do this exercise in groups of three or four.

IV. Review and Application of Stages of Mediation   (1½–2 hours)

A review of the stages of mediation and additional skills practice are the most frequently requested agendas for the first advanced workshop.

Advance Preparation

Make sufficient copies of the role-play "The Student and the Jazz Musician" in Chapter Eight (use "Neighborhood Conflict: Children and Dogs" if you used "The Student and the Jazz Musician" in the basic workshop). Provide each small group with markers and a flipchart.

A number of additional role-plays follow the case studies; many of the storytelling role-plays can be used in this exercise with a brief explanation of the context. Other sources for role-plays are the Jossey-Bass Web site, www.josseybass.com/peaceskills, and the second edition of *The Role-Play Book: 41 Hypothetical Situations* by Ron Mock (Akron, Pa.: Mennonite Conciliation Service, 1997).

Objectives

- To review the stages of mediation and the application of mediation skills

- To sharpen co-mediation skills

A. Review of the Stages (30–40 minutes) It is possible to review the stages of mediation by referring to Exhibit 3.1 in the *Peace Skills* Manual. However, it is more engaging to use the following design.

1. Post four large sheets of newsprint around the room. Title them "Introduction," "Storytelling," "Problem Solving," and "Agreement." If desired, place the goals of "Provide safety," "Offer understanding," "Build joint ownership," and "Seek sustainability" under the respective titles.

2. Divide participants into four groups, sending one group to each of the pages. Ask each group to develop a set of components for its assigned stage. (*The members of the "Problem Solving" group may need additional help from the leadership team, but let them first work alone.*)

3. Have the small groups describe the steps or critical components of their assigned mediation stage to the full group. (Allow five minutes for each presentation.)

4. Ask the full group for additional suggestions. The leadership team may also need to provide additional material in each of the four stages.

B. Application (1 hour) "The Student and the Jazz Musician" is an uncomplicated role-play. Beginning mediators should be able to complete it in thirty to forty-five minutes.

People often learn as much about the mediation process from careful observation as from direct involvement. If there is a large enough group, suggest that some of the participants take the role of a coach, observing the parties and mediators and leading the debriefing session. While the teams are preparing for the role-play, discuss with the coaches the guidelines presented in "Debriefing Role-Plays and Using Coaches with Small Groups" in Chapter One.

1. Consider having the neighbor-mediator ask another neighbor to serve as co-mediator in order to offer additional practice in this skill.

2. Give the parties and mediation teams sufficient time to prepare for their roles.

3. Monitor the role-plays to allow sufficient time for small and plenary group debriefings, keeping in mind that debriefing is usually more important than completing the mediation.

4. Focus the large group debriefing on areas where most groups had difficulty—for example, if the parties became more polarized or if the mediators had difficulty identifying the parties' issues in nonjudgmental terms. Post and discuss the issues selected by each team.

C. Cross-Cultural Implications Discuss how and why the role-play conflict might be different if ethnic diversities were involved, particularly if you focused on cross-cultural communication earlier in the day. Ask the following questions:

- What if the student were Asian and the musician were African American? What if the student were Hispanic and the musician were Anglo?

- What are the implications of cultural or ethnic differences for the co-mediators?

V. Additional Topics

Advanced groups may request additional attention to almost any aspect of the basic workshop. Use creativity and the group's life experiences with handling conflict as two of your most valuable resources. The following suggestions may stimulate fresh ways to address these topics:

A. Getting Parties to the Table   (30–60 minutes)

(Refer to the Peace Skills *Manual, Chapter Four.)* Use as a context a conflict that is taking place in the community and that is open to mediation.

1. In several fishbowl role-plays, assign one person to be a representative of one party and another to take the role of a peacebuilder who tries to explore the possibility of mediation or dialogue with other parties.

2. After each pair finishes, first give the role-players and then the full group time to evaluate the discussion.

3. After three or four brief role-plays, have the group begin to build a set of "dos and don'ts" for getting parties to the table. List these on newsprint. *(This discussion can be particularly insightful in a multicultural group.)*

B. Tools for Breaking Impasse   (45–60 minutes)

(Refer to the Peace Skills *Manual, Chapter Eight for the next three approaches.)*

1. Dealing with Overresponsibility The tendency to become overresponsible is very strong with many people learning to mediate, and it is often difficult for them to recognize. The trainer or leadership team should look for opportunities to call this to the group's attention and invite discussion. For example, a trainer may notice in a role-play that the mediators have been demonstrating overresponsibility, coming up with all the ideas for resolution, pushing the parties to accept certain solutions, and acting in ways that suggest they feel greater urgency for resolving the situation than the parties do.

Meanwhile, the parties are becoming increasingly intransigent. The trainer might invite comment by asking the parties how they felt about the mediators, whether they felt themselves moving toward flexibility or away from it, or who seemed to be assuming the most responsibility for the situation. Ask the mediators to comment on whether they felt they were making headway with the parties and what their feelings were as they mediated.

2. Dealing with Impasse Ask people to tell about techniques or strategies that they have found effective in dealing with impasse. Summarize these on newsprint. As an alternative, put people in small groups to decide one important strategy for effectively breaking impasse. Each group should prepare a five-minute skit to present the use of this strategy in a conflict situation. This is often much more interesting and insightful than simply conducting a theoretical discussion.

3. Using Caucus This skill is usually not introduced until the end of a basic workshop. It provides such an easy way out of difficult moments that learners may rely on it too heavily and never develop other skills for dealing with difficult situations. Here are some ideas for teaching the use of caucus:

a. Ask the group to call out the benefits and dangers of caucus; list these on newsprint. This usually leads to a good discussion of the basic concept of caucus.

b. Demonstrate a short role-play of caucus in front of the full group and then discuss it. Use a role-play the group has already used, or pick a difficult conflict that is currently in the news. Set up the role-play by explaining that key leaders in the conflict have agreed to meet with a mediator. The mediation session has reached impasse, and the mediator has decided to caucus with the parties.

c. Begin the role-play with both parties in joint session with the mediator so that the group can observe how the mediator makes the shift from joint session to caucus. If any agreements are worked out during the caucus discussion, the mediator should continue with the task of bringing the parties together again and checking for agreement in the presence of both.

VI. Local Application   (30 minutes)

Many groups use at least a part of the advanced workshop to discuss organization and details of future workshops, the formation of peacebuilding networks, and direct involvement in specific community issues.

Section Three

Community Conflict Case Studies, Role-Plays, and Sacred Text Studies

The final paragraphs of Chapter Two contain a brief synopsis of each of the case studies in Chapter Seven: "Beyond the Battle," "Call to Prayer," "Giving Thanks," and "Lord of the Dance." The section in Chapter Two titled "Selecting the Right Case" suggests guidelines for matching the case study with your workshop goals and participants' interests. Although the context for "Lord of the Dance" is a religious congregation, each of these cases could be discussed in a secular or religious setting.

Workshop leaders may copy the cases from the Leaders' Guide or the Web site and provide them to the participants. The one-page handout "What Cases Are and How to Study Them" should accompany a case mailed to participants in advance. If participants are not able to read the selected case prior to the workshop, be sure to allow sufficient time during the workshop for everyone to read it carefully before the case discussion.

The Teaching Notes that follow each case are not for duplication or distribution to participants prior to the case discussion. These notes suggest one of many ways for workshop leaders to organize the discussion. Leaders should study Chapter Two, the sections titled "Presenting the Case" and "Teaching the Case," for more detailed teaching suggestions.

Chapter One and the course designs in Chapters Four and Five offer numerous suggestions for using the role-plays that follow each case study and the independent role-plays in Chapter Eight. The role-plays are formatted to enable workshop leaders to photocopy them easily and divide the roles or profiles to give to individual participants.

The sample questions, applications to life, and the background information on the sacred texts presented in Chapter Nine were developed to address particular themes in a workshop experience. A brief synopsis of each of these studies—"Recognition and Listening," "Healing and Reconciliation," "Forgiveness and Enemies," and "Justice and Freedom"—is at the end of Chapter Three. With the exception of the extensive text from Genesis (Healing and Reconciliation), each of the texts is printed for leaders to duplicate and hand out to participants.

Leaders should study in advance Chapter Three (the sections titled "Approaches to Studying Sacred Texts" and "Guidelines for Group Sacred Text Study") for detailed teaching suggestions. We encourage workshop leaders to adapt these questions and select additional passages from authoritative and sacred texts to meet the needs and goals of their own groups, to incorporate their own insights, and to develop their own questions. In some communities, especially in a faith-oriented workshop, each session might include the study of a text. In other workshops, sacred texts may not be a component at all.

CHAPTER 7

Community Conflict Case Studies

 CHAPTER TWO, "Case Studies in Conflict Transformation," offers workshop leaders detailed suggestions for presenting and teaching these and other case studies. Additional case studies are posted on the Jossey-Bass Web site, www.josseybass.com/peaceskills.

BEYOND THE BATTLE

Case Study

Martha Jones felt an uncharacteristic knot in the pit of her stomach as she thought about tomorrow night. Her first meeting as president of the Springfield Board of Education could well be another battle—this time over the board's response to escalating violence in the schools.

Springfield was a city of two hundred thousand people, with another three hundred thousand living in the Greater Springfield region. The city was surrounded by highly diverse areas of suburban wealth and rural poverty. It had one of the largest united (urban-suburban) school systems in the state and was among the thirty poorest cities in the country. More than half of the thirty-five thousand urban public schoolchildren—55 percent black, 24 percent Latino, and 18 percent white—qualified for free or reduced-price meals. Although there had been some increase in the minority population in the wealthy suburbs, the population there was still predominantly white. The local newspaper had run several features on the effects of the

This case study was written by Robert A. Evans and Alice Frazer Evans and appears in the *Journal of the Association for Case Teaching*, volume 5. Copyright ©1993 the Case Study Institute. Used by permission. The names of all persons and places in this case have been disguised to protect the privacy of individuals involved.

recession and on residents who had lost their jobs in the manufacturing, high-tech, and service industries. Most stories highlighted the residents' feelings of vulnerability and anxiety. A new city administration was recently elected on a platform of political, economic, and educational reform.

Martha Jones was a lifelong resident of the predominantly black south side of Springfield. She had been a teacher in the Springfield school system for more than thirty years. Ironically, she was one of the original plaintiffs in a twenty-five-year-old desegregation suit against the board on which she now served. Because the city's court-ordered desegregation plan of the early 1970s failed to bring about integrated schools, Martha still refused to sign off on the suit. As a child advocate and an activist teacher, she was often at war with the Board of Education. Public dissatisfaction with the schools had ensured her election to the board three years ago after she retired from her teaching position. Last month she was elected to the presidency by a narrow margin.

Martha believed that the city and the board had to find a way beyond their battles. "Our first priority was the children" is her plea. But she knew that declaring priorities was easier than moving the school system ahead in a positive manner. After years of public fights about the budget and the suspension and forced resignation of the last superintendent, many residents viewed the board as dysfunctional. Martha knew that it was going to be hard to recover credibility. She also knew that a board and a city polarized by class and race complicated issues.

The board was facing a highly controversial proposal to install expensive metal detectors in the city's two high schools and several junior highs and to hire more trained security guards for all schools. A gang culture had begun to develop in three of the poorest black and Hispanic areas of the city. City police attributed three recent "drive-by" shootings to drug activity. Elementary, junior high, and high school teachers were reporting an increasing number of knives and guns in the schools. A threat by an angry student with a handgun prompted the current proposal for metal detectors. Martha saw that the only funds available for increased security were those that were already budgeted for implementing a hard-won, long-term educational reform program.

The reform program had been generated by a group of parent advocates and followed the guidelines of a national program titled America 2000. The plan focused on high standards and student performance assessment. It also included moving the system from central to local site-based decision making about budget, personnel, curriculum, and new programs such as peer mediation. The parent support group for Springfield 2000 had consulted with the superintendent's office, representatives of teachers' bargaining units, principals, custodians, and members of the Board of Education, including Martha during her first term on the board. Martha had supported the basic concepts of the reform package, and the board passed a motion to budget funds to implement Phase 1 just before city elections.

Martha suspected that election shifts in board membership could mean that she would have the deciding vote on continued support of the reform package. She was reluctant to begin her term as president with business as usual—win-lose tactics through power blocs on the board. But with limited funds, systemic reform was being pitted against immediate needs. "How can we spend for the future when we can't pay for the present?" was a question she had heard more than once. Increased violence and drug use had everyone concerned, if not in a panic. Martha was unsure if this was the best or the worst time to implement systemic reform.

Martha personally contacted the six other board members and received dozens of phone calls during the past week. To prepare for the board meeting, she reviewed her notes from her numerous conversations. Martha looked first at notes from a personal visit and several phone conversations with Sally Thompson, a former president of the Springfield Junior League and now principal parent spokesperson for the reform initiative:

> Springfield 2000 will make systemic changes in the educational system. I know this scares some people. Members of the board, administrators, principles, teachers, staff, and members of the city council and state legislature might lose a little power. However, many of us believe it is the only recourse before the courts enforce another mandatory program to achieve greater integration. The original court plan failed to bring the intended result of better education for all. The magnet schools thrived; the rest of the system deteriorated, leading to more white flight to the suburbs and private schools. The community needs time to build consensus for a comprehensive system of quality education. The proposal focuses on long-term transformation, not a quick fix.

Sally told Martha in one conversation:

> I acknowledge there is an increase of violence in the city. I also believe that fear is a more powerful motivator than excellence. I know we are talking about using seriously limited funds for restructuring and educational reform versus security. But you need to remember that we worked on this proposal for three years with several hundred people in the school system and the community. There was an emerging consensus that we need accountability

that focuses on results. Site-based decision making requires ongoing involvement in our schools by both parents and the business community. Decentralization of authority is the only way we will ever reclaim local ownership and pride in city schools. Direct parent and community involvement is also the best way to address the violence and fear.

Serious concern about violence prompted comments from Thomas Jackson, a three-term board member and local businessman who had been Martha's ally on a number of issues. "Until we get back control of our schools and streets from the gangs, reform doesn't mean a thing," he declared in a conversation outside church on Sunday morning. "We have students being shot by other students on the grounds of the school. We can't wait around for conflict resolution skills. We need conflict control with metal detectors in every school, more security guards to confiscate weapons, and policemen with dogs to locate drugs."

Thomas had a different perspective on the school desegregation suit. He confessed to Martha his deep discomfort with the prospect of court intervention that might bus his children into the white suburbs:

> It may be "safer" out there, but it is devoid of the African American values of respect and reverence that in my youth in the ghetto encouraged the whole black community to act as parents. Segregated schools are not the primary threat to quality education. It is radically unequal access to funds, services, and opportunity. These white elitist reformers pushing for state-supported, regional reforms are not terrified to walk *their* streets at night or attend after-school events. We have some white tenured teachers in our black schools who are not only afraid of our kids but actually despise them. With this tenure system, teachers have no accountability to the community, only to union rules. I am going to fight to put money into immediate protection, not into this pretense of long-term systems change.

"I am suspicious of reforms that pile more expectation on teachers to save our kids and the city," Michael Gonzales, president of the Springfield Teachers Federation, told Martha at a reception honoring the Teacher of the Year.

> A segregated school system is a result of segregated neighborhoods sustained by economic inequality. The crisis in this city is about poverty and the subsequent decline of the family system. Fifty percent of black children, 30 percent of Hispanic children, and

20 percent of the white children in our school system are living with one parent, usually a woman who is either unemployed or underemployed. Behind these figures are high divorce rates, teen pregnancy, and out-of-wedlock babies. The youth culture promoted on TV reduces respect for authority and promotes violence and craving to have things the media advertise. Our city's race relations have gone to hell. We live in almost completely isolated worlds of dominant and minority cultures. We meet only in the workplace, and even there we carefully keep our distance.

Our teachers are concerned about safety and job security in a frightening economy. Many of us support elements of the reform package, particularly more control over curriculum. But we feel dumped on by a community that expects us to solve the problems parents can't or won't face. Teachers are uneasy about additional burdens of team teaching, integrated disciplines, and new topics like conflict resolution added to their teaching responsibilities. Earlier school reforms focused on minimal student competence, based on statewide testing. This approach pushed teachers to teach for tests rather than develop individual student abilities. This reform proposal for performance-based student outcome seems more promising. But the bottom line is, no matter where they live, people are afraid of violence and drugs—for themselves and their children. Martha, most teachers will support funds for security measures at the cost of long-term reform because they are directly affected by the violence.

John Stewart, the CEO of one of the city's largest corporations, cornered Martha at one of the few social events attended by both whites and African Americans—a dinner celebrating the contributions of Martin Luther King Jr.:

Martha, the community has high hopes that as the new president of the board, you'll be able to bring this destructive feuding to an end. Our goal of regional economic renewal can't be realized without school reform. We have a beautiful, historical city that many firms find attractive until they look at the schools. They ask if we can equip a workforce that is able to cope with the new technological and competitive era we are entering. Let's be candid. You were a good teacher in an increasingly dysfunctional system. Potential employees who visit our city, often committed to public education, wonder where to put their children. They aren't merely fleeing to the suburbs but to private and parochial schools. Many advocate a school voucher system, hoping for some return on their tax dollars and some choice in their children's education. You know I still support the public school system, but my children were fortunate to be in magnet schools, and it was tough even there.

My corporation supports educational reform. Corporate funds are tight now, but we'll put money into the reform program to support corporate community volunteers and promote businesses adopting specific schools. Ultimately, however, the state legislature holds the purse strings for poor urban communities. The increasing violence and especially the apparent inability of city schools to deliver on student outcomes make it harder to justify the investment. School systems like Dade County are expanding their conflict resolution program in the midst of one of the most violent urban areas in the country. The program is already paying off with reduced conflict in the schools. This is just one of many reasons why the reform package must continue to have top priority. But if the board retreats from reform to fund a short-term security system or, God forbid, higher teachers' salaries, that may be the last straw. The city won't get another chance for reform with the base of community support we apparently have now. The board can't continue to fight like jackasses and make every vote a four-to-three political power play. Accountability for all is essential; citizens can no longer avoid appropriate critiques of incompetent performance by students, teachers, or city or school administrators, be they white, black, or Latino, for fear of being called racist. Accountability is a pillar of reform.

Martha glanced at the clock over the kitchen table where she was working. Time is running out, she thought, for Springfield and for me. The security resolution was already on the agenda of tomorrow's Board of Education meeting, and the forces were lining up for the battle. In interviews, the new school superintendent supported the educational reform process. However, Martha was uncertain how she would respond to the various political pressures that were bound to come. How blessed it would feel to be beyond the battle of security versus reform. What kind of leadership was required of an old warhorse, she wondered. When the phone rang, Martha realized how much she needed peace and quiet to think this through, not more pressure from her friends at the union or in the community.

Teaching Notes

Objectives of the Case Discussion

- To begin building a listening and learning community
- To identify sources and types of case conflict
- To analyze parties and stakeholders for workshop role-plays
- To gain practice in distinguishing demands from interests and needs
- To sharpen skills for developing short- and long-term goals and strategies
- To increase interest and energy in the workshop

Reminder: The case is true, disguised, and decision-oriented. Beyond correctly stating factual information, there are no right or wrong answers.

Case Discussion

I. Context and Issues   (30 minutes)

A. Quickly identify the facts in the case that describe the city of Springfield (*size of population, unified urban-suburban school system, economic recession,* and so forth).

B. Discuss the causes and contributing factors that led to the potential impasse on the Springfield Board of Education in funding either long-range reform or security (*class and racial divisions, lack of communication, increased violence, budget constraints*).

C. Use the RIVIRS diagram in Figure 2.1 of this Leaders' Guide to assist with the analysis.

II. Parties and Stakeholders   (30 minutes)
(*Save a record of this discussion.*)

A. Parties to the Conflict Identify each party, one at a time. List and discuss their characteristics.

Party	Position	Interests/Needs	Feelings
Martha Jones, *Board of Education president, veteran teacher*	Undecided	Children, pro-reform, image of board	Anxious

Sally Thompson, *Springfield 2000, Junior League*	Reform	Local control, educational excellence	Fearful, threatened, protective
Thomas Jackson, *school board member, businessman*	Security	African American values, racism, fear in black community, funding equity	Angry, concerned, anxious about children
Michael Gonzales, *president of teachers union*	Security	Poverty, family values, divided city, teachers' job security	Troubled, burdened, torn
John Stewart, *corporation CEO*	Reform	Economic renewal, safe schools, accountability, able workforce	Worried, anxious, committed

B. Stakeholders Identify groups or individuals who could have an impact on board action or long-term resolution of case problems but have not been identified as a party to the deliberations *(children, police, new school superintendent, state taxpayers).*

III. Alternatives: Process, Goals, Strategies   (15–20 minutes)

Martha wants to move the board "beyond the battle" of win-lose decision making. She has already spoken with each board member.

1. What strategies should she use for the board meeting?

2. Identify specific strategies for meeting short-term goals and long-term goals, especially those that might address relationships and structures. *(Use a group role-play or small group discussions. See alternatives under "Teaching the Case" in Chapter Two.)*

IV. Resources   (10–15 minutes)

A. What resources can Martha call on? (For example, *extra time, other sources for security, common concerns for children*)

B. When Martha (or another person) facilitates the next Board of Education meeting, what personal skills are needed? *(listening, patience, balanced support of parties)*

Role-Play #1: Paraphrasing

Facilitator   Jorge Sanchez

Parties   Thomas Jackson, John Stewart

Case Update   Martha Jones was able to get the Board of Education to postpone the vote on appropriating long-range funds for security measures. The board formed the Security Task Force to gather information and seek funding sources. In the days immediately following the board meeting, however, public debate began to escalate between Thomas Jackson and John Stewart, who took opposing sides on the use of board funds. Martha knows both men well and was concerned that their positions not become further entrenched. She visited with them separately to encourage them to meet and discuss their differences privately. Because Martha is the board's president and a close friend of Mr. Jackson, she asked Jorge Sanchez to facilitate the meeting. He is a Springfield City Council member, known and trusted by both Jackson and Stewart.

Profile: Jorge Sanchez

You are a city councilman. John Stewart and Thomas Jackson have each made public statements that reveal their strong differences about the security-versus-reform debate. You know both men well and are deeply concerned about increasing tensions in the Springfield community. Having two prominent businessmen, one white and the other black, in open disagreement only further divides the city. Jackson and Stewart both agree to meet privately with you to see if they can find some way to talk about their differences. You have invited them to meet in your study. While facilitating the meeting, consider the following:

1. Be clear that the meeting's goal is to reach better understanding, not resolution of any issues.

2. Your role is to facilitate their discussion, not to take sides.

3. Ask both to suggest and agree to some basic "ground rules," such as no interruptions and brevity.

4. Get agreement on who speaks first.

5. Paraphrase and summarize their points to build trust and calm their anger or anxiety.

Profile: Thomas Jackson

You are a successful African American businessman, committed to the city and the promotion of strong family values for your children. If the city schools had the same funds as suburban schools, there would be no need to talk of busing inner-city children from their neighborhoods for equal education. Busing children to the white suburbs severs critical Latino and African American ties of family and identity. These are also threatened by the dominant number of white teachers in the Springfield system who have no understanding of cultures other than their own. You are deeply concerned about the growing violence in the city and see the root causes as growing unemployment, increasing poverty, and increasing drug trade. These are linked to businesses that are moving out of the city and middle-class whites, who are the primary purchasers of the drugs.

You have known Jorge Sanchez for a number of years and respect his wisdom and understanding of the city. He is not only your elected councilman but also your friend. Because you are uncomfortable about the public rift between yourself and John Stewart, you were quite willing to accept Sanchez's offer to meet with him and Stewart. You hope that Sanchez can help Stewart understand the real issues of the city instead of carping on narrow, elite images of "long-term reform." There won't be any children or teachers in the schools to reform unless the violence can be stopped.

Profile: John Stewart

You are the CEO of a national corporation with headquarters in Springfield. Recently, several people turned down offers to move up in the corporation if a promotion meant they had to move to Springfield. You feel that conditions in the school system played a significant role in their decisions. You are proud of your city, committed to public education, and convinced that one of the most important ways to improve the climate of the city is through long-term reform of the educational system. You are tired of "quick fixes" and emergencies, which stop progress on this agenda. You and other city leaders invested months in the passage of the Reform 2000 package. You have already solicited the business community for funds to support reform measures. You feel you would undercut progress if you agreed to use reform funds for a short-term "fix" such as electronic metal detectors.

You have known Councilman Jorge Sanchez for a number of years and respect his wisdom and understanding of the city. Because you are uncomfortable about the public rift between yourself and Thomas Jackson, you were quite willing to accept Sanchez's offer to meet with him and Jackson. You hope that Sanchez can help Jackson understand the "big picture" instead of carping on narrow racial issues.

Role-Play #2: Storytelling

Facilitator   Marion Engles

Parties   Michael Gonzales, Sally Thompson

Case Update   It is one week after the Board of Education meeting. The board's Security Task Force has not yet issued a report. Leaders of the Teachers Federation are becoming anxious after hearing rumors that the board was going to support reserving the allocated funds for the reform package and, having no other available funds, would not immediately address issues of security. The Teachers Federation served notice that it may be forced to call for a strike unless additional police are assigned and metal detectors are installed in two weeks. Michael Gonzales, as head of the federation, publicly supports his teachers' demands. Sally Thompson, chair of a recently formed group called Parents' Alliance for School Reform, is deeply concerned that the Teachers Federation will pressure the board to appropriate long-term reform funds to provide safety measures. Gonzales and Thompson have argued publicly about their differences. Both parties accept Martha Jones's suggestion that they meet informally with Marion Engles, a skilled community mediator.

Profile: Marion Engles

You are a Springfield community leader trained in conflict resolution skills. You have been asked by your good friend Martha Jones to help informally mediate a growing dispute between two factions led by Sally Thompson and Michael Gonzales, both of whom you know. You invite Michael and Sally to meet informally in your office. Though you may not reach any agreements, you hope to get them talking to each other before their positions harden or become more extreme. Remember that they may be anxious and suspicious of each other. Your first goal is to provide safety; your second goal is understanding. While facilitating the meeting, consider the following approach.

Introduction

1. Welcome them and explain the process and goals for the meeting.
2. Clarify your role as facilitator.
3. Get agreement on basic ground rules, such as not interrupting each other.
4. Ask how each party would prefer to be addressed (for example, "Michael" or "Mr. Gonzales"?).

Storytelling

1. Have both sides tell their story.
2. Use positive paraphrasing to build trust and calm anger or anxiety. If necessary, use paraphrasing to "launder" any harsh language.
3. Rather than focus on their demands, use open questions or leading statements to help them identify their underlying interests and primary concerns.
4. Listen for and identify common concerns and specific areas of disagreement.
5. When the parties are comfortable enough, "release" them to speak to each other. Look for *their* suggestions.

You would feel some real progress if you could help Sally Thompson and Michael Gonzales gain a better understanding of each other's positions and identify areas of common concern and specific disagreements.

Profile: Michael Gonzales

You are the elected president of the Springfield Teachers Federation. Although a committee was formed to work on security issues at the last Board of Education meeting, there was no formal vote on funding for new security measures. Many of your teachers fear that the board will preserve the full reform package and will ignore the issue of security. Your teachers are increasingly afraid in their classrooms and feel that unless the board members are aware of the severity of the situation, they will not respond.

The day of the Teachers Federation meeting, one week after the board meeting, a teacher confiscated a switchblade that had fallen out of a student's pocket. At this meeting, the teachers voted to call for a strike in two weeks if additional police were not assigned and metal detectors not installed by that time. You know that many teachers agree with the long-range goals of the 2000 plan and that others will be satisfied with *any* clear response by the board regarding their security. However, after a public confrontation with Sally Thompson following the board meeting, you feel that the only way the Sally Thompsons from the suburbs will understand the teachers' situation is to threaten to strike. You have agreed to meet with Marion Engles and Sally Thompson because you trust Marion and because you know that ultimately you need the support of the community to make a difference in the schools.

Profile: Sally Thompson

You are a parent and a strong advocate of the Springfield 2000 program. Although there was no official vote at the last Board of Education meeting, a committee was formed to work on security issues. You are unsure at this point if the board will still support the full, long-range reform package and honor the previously voted allocation of funds. A group of parents, concerned that pressure from teachers would force the board to appropriate Springfield 2000 funds for immediate installation of metal detectors, formed the Parents' Alliance and elected you as chair.

You are convinced that the implementation of the long-range plan, including parent involvement and peer mediation programs, is the best way to improve the school system. You are also deeply concerned about potential violence in the schools and are willing to work with the teachers on some immediate responses. However, you are not willing to abandon hard-won, long-term initiatives to meet short-term needs in the costly, dramatic way the teachers are demanding. You have agreed to meet with Marion Engles—a community mediator—and Michael Gonzales because you trust Marion and because you know that ultimately you need the cooperation of the teachers to make the long-range plan work.

Role-Play #3: Multiparty Facilitation

A fishbowl approach is best for this role-play. Prepare large name tags for the eight principal parties, and have a newsprint easel and markers available for the facilitators. Divide the participants into four small groups, by either assigning the groups or having the participants select their roles (meeting facilitators, Teachers Federation, Parents' Alliance, or Board of Education). Have copies of the appropriate role available for all participants in each group. *(Refer to the basic workshop, Day Two, Section XVII.B, "Multiparty Facilitation Role-Play," for detailed suggestions about conducting and debriefing this role-play.)*

Note that the parties will not be able to reach any agreements in the time allotted for this role-play.

Facilitators   A respected team identified by the new school superintendent

Parties   Teachers Federation: Michael Gonzales and a teacher
Parents' Alliance for School Reform: John Stewart and Sally Thompson
Board of Education: Thomas Jackson and Martha Jones

Objectives
- To apply some of what participants have learned in the workshop
- To experience the potential and challenges of multiparty facilitation
- To have fun with the different roles.

Case Update   Three weeks after the Board of Education meeting and before the board's Security Task Force makes any formal announcements, a knife-wielding student threatens a high school teacher. In the midst of the ensuing publicity, the new school superintendent decides to go outside the school system for a two-person team to facilitate a meeting between some of the major parties. All parties agree to send two representatives to meet with the facilitators. One representative from each party will begin with a two-minute opening statement. The parties have taken the following public positions. *(Post these on the board or newsprint.)*

Teachers Federation (represented by Michael Gonzales and a teacher): The teachers' union calls for a strike if security devices and additional police are not in place by the end of the week.

Parents' Alliance for School Reform (represented by Sally Thompson and John Stewart): This newly formed parents and business coalition will sue the Board of Education if it gives in to the union's demands and appropriates reform funds to purchase metal detectors.

Board of Education (represented by Martha Jones and Thomas Jackson): The board reports that the members are making progress on the issues and should be free from harassment to do their job.

Profile: Meeting Facilitator

You are one of the co-facilitators of a meeting between representatives of (1) the Teachers Federation, (2) the Parents' Alliance for School Reform, and (3) the Board of Education. You have done a great deal of advance preparation for this meeting, and all of the parties have agreed to meet with you and to abide with the ground rules established.

As a co-facilitator, you are clear that you will not be making decisions for the group. At this meeting, you hope to facilitate the group's conversation, build understanding for opposing positions, and lay the groundwork for mutually agreeable resolutions. You want to look for ways to strengthen the parties' relationships and empower them to address some of the "causal and contributing factors" that surfaced during the case analysis.

Things to Decide in Advance

- The room arrangement

- Your opening comments (including any ground rules)

- The order in which one member of each team presents a two-minute introductory statement

Your Strategies

- To help the parties listen to one another by paraphrasing their concerns

- To help the group identify common ground and the most critical issues that need to be addressed

- To post the issues and select one to discuss

- To progress as far as possible in the time allotted

Profile: Michael Gonzales

You are the president of the Teachers Federation. Shortly before the most recent meeting of the federation, a knife-wielding student threatened one of your high school teachers. At that meeting, *the teachers voted to call a strike unless security devices and additional police are in place by the end of the week.* You believe that the Board of Education and the Parents Alliance for School Reform do not realize the level of the teachers' anxiety and fear, not only for themselves but also for the students. The teachers are also angry about the obvious lack of concern by the Parents' Alliance, which focuses only on tomorrow and ignores the realities of today. You privately know that many teachers are against a strike, but you will need concrete plans for immediate action to avert a majority vote to strike.

You were asked to develop a two-minute opening statement for a multi-party facilitation. You are aware that the two other parties, the Board of Education and the Parents' Alliance, will have two representatives at the meeting. You decided just last night to bring to the meeting the high school teacher who was threatened. You have asked her to give the opening statement.

Profile: Sally Thompson and John Stewart

Your team represents the Parents' Alliance for School Reform (Sally Thompson, chair) and the corporate community (John Stewart, Alliance member). While you are concerned about the increase of weapons in the schools, you believe that the teachers' demands for expensive metal detectors and a police presence are exaggerated and may be an attempt to derail implementation of long-term reform. You also believe that this strong-arm approach to deal with a few students would further erode the image of the school system. Parental involvement, better discipline in the classrooms, and conflict resolution training—all of which are part of the Springfield 2000 plan—would provide a better, more sustainable response. You have both made public statements that *the Parents' Alliance will sue the Board of Education if it gives in to the teachers' demands and uses previously allocated, long-term reform funds to buy metal detectors.*

You are both *privately* willing to help raise funds for less visible forms of security, but you are not willing to give in to the pressure tactics introduced by the teachers. One of you needs to develop a two-minute opening statement for the multiparty facilitation.

Profile: Martha Jones and Thomas Jackson

You are a team selected to represent the Board of Education. You believe that good progress is being made toward getting assistance from the Springfield business community for alternative approaches and funding to resolve the security issues, but the threatened teachers' strike for immediate implementation could derail these plans.

You agree that direct action must be taken to address the increase in weapons and a growing sense of insecurity in some schools, but these are issues for the new school superintendent and the board to handle. In addition, a strike would endanger many children whose parents work outside the home and would further erode the image of the school system. You are also upset with public statements being made by the Parents' Alliance about suing the Board of Education if you "give in" to the teachers' demands to use Springfield 2000 funds to implement security measures. To move forward with both security and reform, the board needs the full support and cooperation of teachers, parents, and community businesses. However, for long-term credibility, the board cannot afford to give in to the threats of either the Teachers Federation or the Parents' Alliance. Your declared position is that *the Security Task Force is making progress; the community needs to cool down and let you do your job.* One of you needs to develop a two-minute opening statement for the multiparty facilitation.

CALL TO PRAYER

Case Study

Kareem Rashid put down the telephone with a sigh. Mary Burns was clearly upset. She had made her first call to him almost a week ago to request his assistance with a conflict situation in one of her departments. Kareem had agreed and met with several people in the office, particularly with Shakir Akhmed, to gain a better understanding of the problems. However, at this point he saw the situation headed toward deeper mistrust and possibly a legal challenge by Shakir that could spill over into the whole organization and even the community.

The conflict was in one of the four departments of Columbus County Social Services. The poor of Columbus had not benefited from the economic boom of the late 1990s. Although the county included wealthy rural and suburban communities, the city of 150,000 people had large areas with vacant lots and abandoned apartment buildings. Unemployment and underemployment, particularly among African American and Latino residents, was high. In the aftermath of congressional cuts to welfare, county job placement programs were struggling to locate jobs for welfare recipients who would soon lose benefits. In his role as director of a nonprofit community service agency that worked closely with the county, Kareem was well acquainted with the area's social problems, including hunger and homelessness. He was also keenly aware of the pressures on overloaded caseworkers in social services and divisions in a city where contact between people of different races, cultures, classes, or religions was often limited to their place of employment.

Kareem recalled his original conversation with Mary. She said that she called Kareem not only because she respected and trusted him but because he was an African American Muslim like Shakir, and she felt sure he could "get Shakir to be more reasonable."

As director of County Social Services, Mary had recently hired Jose Ricardo as supervisor of the combined department of housing and employment. She told Kareem she was "particularly pleased to get Ricardo, who had exceptional credentials and the ability to relate well to the agency's growing Hispanic constituency—now nearly 50 percent of our clients." Mary noted that a master's degree was required for the job. Jose did not have the degree, but he was enrolled in a program and had almost completed his coursework.

Mary explained:

> The supervisor's position was vacant when Shakir Akhmed was hired seven months ago. He moved into the corner office during the summer when several of us were on vacation. I was sure he realized that this was the supervisor's office, but when I told him yesterday that he had to move, he exploded. I first thought the problem was professional jealousy. Shakir is as experienced as Jose, and he has a fine record with his clients. However, he simply does not have the educational qualifications for this supervisory position.
>
> What really threw me is that Shakir has threatened to file a claim with the state for discrimination based on freedom of religion. This is ridiculous. I know that he's a Muslim; this is the main reason I never call staff meetings for Friday when he goes to the mosque. It's true that he had to move into one of the smaller offices, but it was the only one available. In terms of trading offices, the rest of the department staff are overloaded with cases of people who have no homes and no jobs, much less an office! It's not fair to ask one of these busy people, all of whom have been here longer, to pack their files and move their office on somebody's whim. I want Jose Ricardo to feel welcome when he arrives next Wednesday, and I sure don't want the situation to escalate to a public suit.

Kareem was clear with Mary that he didn't see his role as convincing Shakir of anything. However, he would be glad to come and speak to Shakir and some of his colleagues if this was acceptable to Mary. Mary agreed, and Kareem called Shakir that afternoon for an appointment.

Kareem had known Shakir Akhmed for a number of years. Now in his late forties, Shakir had been raised as a Christian. He had been an avid reader of the Bible and taught Sunday school. The only time he lived outside of Columbus was during a tour of duty with the U.S. Army. He attended a local college for two and a half years before taking a job in the corporate world. Kareem recalled Shakir coming to him to learn more about Islam soon after downsizing phased out Shakir's position. At the time he was thirty-two years old. Kareem felt that he was searching for his identity and his heritage. Shakir began studying Islam and the Qur'an with the same intensity he had studied Christianity and the Bible. A year later, he changed his name from James Porter to Shakir Akhmed.[1] However, it was not until years later that Shakir converted to Islam.

When he met Shakir the following afternoon in his new office, Kareem briefly shared what Mary had said and asked for Shakir's perspective. Shakir shook his head and replied slowly:

> For a middle-aged white woman, Mary Burns isn't such a bad director, but she certainly doesn't know anything about Islam. I became a Muslim because the leaders I admire most are like you—people who live out their faith and uphold the tenets of Islam with discipline and consistency. This is why it is so important for me to maintain the discipline of daily prayers and reciting verses of the Qur'an. My former office was close to the washroom for purification before prayer. I had a place to hang my prayer rug, a door for privacy, and enough room to not only stand and bow but also to kneel and prostrate myself before God as a sign of my submission to His will.[2] Now look around at this cubicle! Though the partitions are relatively soundproof, there is no real privacy in here. It's so cramped there's not enough room to pray unless I move the desk to the wall and take the client's chair out into the hallway!
>
> You noted Mary Burns's suspicion that I was angry about not getting the supervisor's job. I admit to being initially upset by Ricardo's hiring. Like me, he doesn't have the required master's degree. I have as much experience in other agencies as he does, and I know the city like the back of my hand. Frankly, I think this guy should go back to Puerto Rico where he came from to deal with the problems there. But this isn't the source of my complaint against Burns and department policies. It's about religion.
>
> I don't experience tension with most Christians. Although I have rousing debates with my sister about my faith, I travel crosstown every Sunday to drive my mother to her Methodist church. I believe Jesus was God's prophet as well as Muhammad. We both know that more Muslims believe in the Virgin Birth than Christians do! The people I have trouble with are those who don't respect people of other faiths. I am convinced that I was moved into a space that imposes severe restrictions on my practices of faith because I am a Muslim in a dominant Christian culture.

At Mary's suggestion, and with Shakir's knowledge, Kareem then spoke privately with other members of the office staff. June Baxter met him with a hesitant handshake, which Kareem felt belied her warm smile. A white woman about ten years younger than Shakir, June said she and her family had moved to the area a year ago. "Before our move, I was a social worker in a much smaller town. Shakir was a tremendous help in getting me acquainted with issues in Columbus."

June expressed surprise about Shakir's interpretation of his office move. She said she had felt "really dumb" about her ignorance of Muslim practices. "When I first met him, I put out my hand, and Shakir said that Muslim men don't touch women who aren't related to them.[3] You both wear the same kind of little cap,[4] so I assumed you were a Muslim too. I guess that's why I was taken aback when you offered your hand. Now I feel even dumber. I thought Shakir's prayer rug was a wall decoration! I don't have anything at all against Muslims. Shakir needs to share his concerns and educate us."

It was Friday afternoon before Earl Green was free to meet with Kareem. Earl was an African American who had worked for County Social Services for a number of years. His response was that Shakir needed to "cool it." "Shakir and I have been friends since elementary school. You know as well as I do that you can't live in this city as an African American and not experience discrimination. I guess you feel even more on the margin as a Muslim. Social Services is one of the few agencies in the city openly seeking a diverse staff. Sure, there are some bumps along the way. But I learned a long time ago you got to roll with the punches. It's about survival—not about making statements."

When Kareem returned to share with Shakir his colleagues' perspectives, Shakir turned away from him and spoke sharply:

> You are returning with a litany of excuses from people who don't care enough to even try to understand. My friend Hakem Abdulah is a client of another county department. He is married and has a good job, but his application to become a foster parent was turned down. I am convinced, as he is, that there is not a single reason other than his Muslim faith that led to this determination. He is aware of my situation in this office and has urged me to stand firm. At some point, we have to take a stand for recognition and respect. Nonviolent resistance is at the heart of the civil rights movement, and one of those civil rights is freedom from persecution for religious beliefs. If a legal suit is what it takes for Islam to be respected, then this is where I have to go.

Kareem had tried to call Mary Burns later on Friday but found that she had left the building for a meeting. On Monday morning when Mary returned Kareem's call, she said someone had already contacted her from the education department expressing support for Shakir. "Kareem, I really appreciate your efforts here. I'm open to any and all suggestions for dealing with this as fairly and as quickly as possible."

Kareem responded that he needed "a way to help you good people talk to one another." Mary agreed to his suggestion of offering mediation. Now he needed to sort out the best way to proceed.

Notes

1. Converts to Islam may change their name to a traditional Muslim name if the given name is normally identified as a "Christian" name such as James, John, or Christine. The name change signifies publicly a change in the person. In addition, African Americans who consider their family name as one given in slavery may change their name as a sign of African identity and recovery of their own name.

2. Devout Muslims practice the Five Pillars (essential principles) of Islam. One of these is *Salat*, praying five times a day: at dawn, noon, afternoon, sunset, and bedtime.

3. Touching between men and women who are not related is constrained in several passages in the Qur'an and the Sunna (writings about the practices of Muhammad). Although social customs follow this practice in the Middle East, it may or may not be followed by Muslims in the United States.

4. The cap, or *kufi*, worn by many Muslim men is part of traditional Muslim culture. Following the example of Muhammad, many men keep their head covered when they pray.

Teaching Notes

Objectives of the Case Discussion

- To begin building a listening and learning community with a focus on interfaith and intercultural communication and understanding
- To identify sources and types of case conflict
- To gain practice in distinguishing demands from interests and needs
- To sharpen skills for developing short- and long-term goals and strategies

Reminder: The case is true, disguised, and decision-oriented. Beyond correctly stating factual information, there are no right or wrong answers.

Case Discussion

I. Context and Issues   **(30 minutes)**

A. Quickly note facts in the case that describe (1) the city of Columbus (for example, *poverty, welfare crisis, racial and cultural divisions*) and (2) County Social Services *(four departments, multicultural, job stress).*

B. Discuss the causes and contributing factors that led to the conflict between Mary Burns and Shakir Akhmed about the office relocation *(misunderstanding, lack of communication, assumption of motives, job-related pressures, religious ignorance or discrimination).*

C. Use the RIVIRS diagram in Figure 2.1 of this Leaders' Guide to analyze the various types of conflict in this case. *(See* Peace Skills *Manual, Chapter Two, "Sources and Types of Conflict," and Leaders' Guide, Chapter Two, "Teaching the Case.")*

II. Parties and Stakeholders   **(30 minutes)**
(Save a record of this discussion.)

A. Kareem Rashid Who is he? What is his role?

B. Parties to the Conflict Identify each party, one at a time. List and discuss their characteristics.

Party	Position	Interests/Needs	Feelings
Mary Burns, *middle-aged, Anglo, supervisor*	No other space available	Equity, funding, good staff relations	Anxious, unsure
Shakir Akhmed, *Muslim convert, advocate for poor, African American*	Wants another office	Respect, recognition of faith demands, equal opportunity	Hurt, angry

Discuss more briefly: Jose Ricardo, June Baxter, Earl Green, Hakem Abdulah

C. Stakeholders Identify groups or individuals who could have an impact on the department's decisions or long-term resolution but have not been identified as a party to the deliberations *(employees in other departments, clients, community, taxpayers).*

III. Alternatives: Process, Goals, and Strategies   (15–20 minutes)

Kareem wants to "help these good people talk to one another."

  1. How can he best accomplish this?

  2. Identify specific approaches to meet short-term and long-term goals.

  3. Which approaches to this conflict might bring constructive change or even transformation?

  4. What principles of a positive process could be shared with the wider community?

IV. Resources   (10–15 minutes)

A. What resources can Kareem call on to achieve the identified goals?

B. If Kareem becomes facilitator of a meeting between Mary, Shakir, or other parties, what skills will he need *(listening, patience, equity)*?

V. Closing

Ask participants to share things they have learned during the discussion about people who are of other faiths and hold perspectives different from their own.

Role-Play

Facilitator

Kareem Rashid *(Note: This role-play can be used effectively to practice "getting parties to the table," as well as paraphrasing and distinguishing between positions and needs/interests. It can also be expanded to include co-workers or to have the facilitator mediate an agreement.)*

Parties

Shakir Akhmed, Mary Burns

Case Update

Mary Burns, director of Columbus County Social Services, and Shakir Akhmed, a social worker in the Employment and Housing Department of the agency, have agreed to meet with Kareem Rashid to discuss their concerns about office relocation.

Profile: Kareem Rashid

You are an African American and have been a practicing Muslim for most of your life. As director of an urban nonprofit service agency, you are a well-known and respected networker and peacebuilder. Mary Burns contacted you after Shakir Akhmed claimed that he was forced to move from his office because of religious persecution. You have met individually with both Burns and Akhmed. They have agreed to meet together with you to share their concerns. While facilitating the meeting, consider the following approach.

Introduction

1. Welcome them, and explain the process and goals for the discussion.

2. Clarify your role.

3. Get agreement on some ground rules, such as respect and not interrupting one another.

4. Get agreement on who speaks first.

Storytelling

1. Have the parties share their perspectives and primary concerns one at a time.

2. "Ignore" their stated positions. Use open questions or statements and paraphrasing to help them raise their underlying needs and interests.

3. Summarize their common concerns, and identify problems or areas of disagreement in neutral terms.

You would feel some real progress if you could help Mary Burns and Shakir Akhmed gain a better understanding of each other's positions and identify areas of common concern and specific disagreements.

Profile: Shakir Akhmed

When you were employed by Columbus County Social Services seven months ago, you were never told that you did not belong in the office where the janitor had placed your boxes of books and personal effects. Now Dr. Burns has forced you to move into a much smaller space to make room for the new department supervisor. She seems convinced that you resisted the move because you are angry that you were not considered for the job of supervisor. She told you that your rejection was because you did not have the necessary degrees. You know that the Puerto Rican man who was hired doesn't have these qualifications either. There was clearly injustice in the hiring process.

However, you have a much greater concern. The new cubicle to which you were assigned allows neither privacy nor space for you to conduct the daily prayers required of a devout Muslim. As an African American, you are used to discrimination, but you will not subject your faith to this kind of insult. When you became a Muslim six years ago, you vowed to practice faithfully the essential principles of Islam. One of these is to pray five times a day. To be forced to pray in a toilet stall—the only other private place in the department—is humiliating.

Dr. Burns and your co-workers may well be seriously ignorant of your faith practices. But ignorance and insensitivity are building blocks of religious intolerance. And intolerance is the root of persecution and hatred. In your work in the city, you are an advocate for poor people who have no voice. Your role is to help them gain dignity through jobs and housing and thus gain a voice to speak for themselves. Too often people of faith think they should not speak out or "make waves." This is the case of your Muslim friend Hakem, who feels he was denied a foster child because he is Muslim. But if oppressed groups are afraid to speak out, they are shoved under the rug or into untenable cubicles. Unless you are given a private place to practice your faith, you will file a claim of discrimination with the state Human Rights Commission.

Profile: Mary Burns

You are the executive director of Columbus County Social Services. Since becoming director four years ago, you have accomplished your goal to develop a staff that reflects the multiracial and multicultural diversity of Columbus. Although you are white, all four department heads are people of color, and the well-qualified staff is culturally and racially diverse. In spite of the challenges this kind of diversity brings, you feel there is generally good morale among the staff. In addition, relationships between staff and clients have improved significantly.

You are deeply concerned about Shakir Akhmed's charge of religious persecution based on your request that he move out of the corner office to make room for the newly hired department supervisor. When Shakir was employed seven months ago, he took the temporarily vacant office while you were on vacation. However, the department supervisor has always occupied this private office in the department. When Jose Ricardo arrives this week, you want him to feel welcome—and not have to negotiate for space.

Shakir's charge of religious persecution is ridiculous! If anything, you have bent over backward to make him feel at home. You do not understand all of the practices of Islam, but you have taken care to avoid calling department staff meetings on Friday when you know he leaves to worship in the mosque. You have a hunch the real problem is that Shakir's nose is out of joint because he was not hired for the supervisor's job. However, his application could not be considered because he does not have the master's degree required for this position. Jose Ricardo is less than three months away from receiving his degree.

The four agency departments are seriously underfunded and understaffed. A public claim of discrimination would not help community relations when you are trying to get additional state funding. You might be able to convince either June Baxter or Earl Green, Shakir's co-workers, to exchange their somewhat larger office with Shakir. However, they are overworked, and you don't want to use their time now to enter the discussion or to move their files into another office.

You value Shakir's ability to relate to African American families. His knowledge of the city has led to numerous previously unlisted housing sites. You don't want to lose a valuable employee, and you certainly don't want a public suit! You hope this meeting with Kareem Rashid, a friend and a well-respected Muslim leader, will convince Shakir to calm down and listen to reason.

GIVING THANKS

Case Study

When Pastor Sam Lee received the call for help from Tom Cho, a prominent Korean American merchant, he realized the situation was serious, but he did not know how serious until he began making inquiries in the community.

During a mid-October meeting, the South End Korean Merchants Association decided to sponsor a block party in South Park to express the merchants' appreciation for the community's business. The merchants, most of whom sold clothing, beauty supplies, shoes, or groceries, voted to accept the proposal to have the party coincide with the American holiday of Thanksgiving. As enthusiasm for the project grew, some merchants offered to contribute money to buy turkeys; others offered products such as clothing or shoes.

The merchants raised enough funds to distribute five hundred turkeys. Two weeks later, the association distributed flyers in the immediate area to announce the date and place of the party—the Saturday before Thanksgiving in South Park. As Cho, president of the Korean Merchants Association, interpreted for Pastor Lee, "We thought this would be a good way to show we appreciate the support of the community."

The following week, to Cho's surprise and distress, another set of flyers appeared in the neighborhood. These flyers called for a boycott of the block party and a protest march against the event. The time and place were identical to those given for the block party. In bold letters the flyers stated: "Korean merchants are bloodsuckers. Kick them out of our neighborhood. They are trying to buy us with their gifts. Come together to protest. Get them out!" The flyers were unsigned.

Many Korean American families who owned and operated stores in the South End, including Tom Cho, attended and lived near Pastor Lee's large Korean church in another part of the city. Though Lee was not surprised to hear from Cho about ethnic tension in the neighborhood, he was deeply concerned about the level of anger in the flyer.

For more than thirty years, the South End had been a stable community of predominantly lower- to middle-income African American residents. The thriving business district near South Park, however, had a wide assortment of small businesses owned and operated by an ethnically diverse group of merchants. Korean Americans had begun establishing small businesses in the area about ten years ago. Most of them had thrived. Almost all the older

This case study was written by Alice Frazer Evans and appeared in the *Journal of the Association for Case Teaching*. Copyright ©1996 the Case Study Institute. Used by permission. The names and places in this case are disguised to protect the privacy of the persons involved.

Korean store owners had emigrated from Korea and still spoke their native language. Several of their children who assisted in the stores had been raised in the United States from childhood and spoke English well.

In response to his conversation with Cho, Pastor Lee decided to visit colleagues in the Black Clergy Association whom he had met at a recent series of clergy prayer breakfasts. He also hoped to speak to some of the neighborhood residents.

Reverend Joshua Taylor, pastor of the South End African Methodist Episcopal (AME) Church, welcomed Lee into his office and said he was equally disturbed by the tone of the flyers. He also shared with Lee another side of the situation:

> Throughout the summer, city residents have been fighting the increase of delis that sell cheap forty-ounce bottles of malt liquor. It's true that these sales are legal, but the effect on our neighborhood has been very destructive.
>
> Groups of kids gather to drink on the street corners. This leads to underage drinking, fights, and shootings. Several of these delis are owned by Koreans who seem to have ignored the residents' protests. Suddenly a group of Korean merchants offers free turkeys. Some residents are convinced that the Korean merchants are trying to bribe them to stop the protests and don't care at all about the neighborhood.

Reverend Taylor offered to go with Lee to meet Eli Johnson, an African American businessman and community activist who lived and worked in the South End. When they met, Johnson first reminded Taylor and Lee that at least three years ago the African American community had renamed South Park as Malcolm X Park. He then pointed to Home Deli just a few doors down from his South End store.

> The Korean who owns that deli started selling cheap malt liquor last April against the wishes of the local police and the community residents. The fights on this corner during the past summer were shameful, and the deli owner goes home at night with bags of money. The Korean store owners do not hire the young African Americans in the neighborhood who desperately need jobs; they hire only their family members. These people don't live here and don't want to be a part of our community. We would all be better off if their stores weren't here.

Lee heard a very different perspective from Doris Allen, who lived in the South End and directed a community assistance program. She did not know who sent out the second set of flyers, but she suspected that the protest movement originated from outside the immediate area. "I'm embarrassed and distressed about the flyers. Many people in the South End are angry about the protest. They see the block party as nothing more than a way to say thanks. Moreover, with winter coming, there are poor families who would be glad to have shoes and clothes. A turkey can feed a hungry family for a week."

"We don't need turkeys; we need long-term commitments to raising the living standards in the whole area." Bill Kennedy, president of the South End Business and Residents Association, said he had learned about the Korean merchants' block party at his association's last meeting only after the flyers had been distributed.

Kennedy continued, "At first glance, it sure looks to me like these merchants are trying to buy the community. We have worked successfully with the city to put in flower boxes and upgrade the bus stops and street signs in our business district. We have also been working for months to build cooperation between residents and businesses. The Koreans have not joined our association and did not consult us at all about this party. The last thing we need is an event that increases racial tension."

Pastor Lee also stopped at the South End police district headquarters to speak with Captain Larkin. Larkin acknowledged that only a small percentage of Korean Americans owned area delis that sold liquor:

> As a matter of fact, five delis in my district recently applied for liquor permits, but none of them are owned by Korean Americans. I have been impressed with the Koreans' commitment to neighborhood youth programs and to their churches. However, my officers are supportive of the residents' opposition to liquor sales at these delis, including Home Deli. This is a volatile issue in the neighborhood, and we are concerned about possible violence. At this point, there is no way we can stop the giveaway or the protest, but unless things cool down, I will certainly assign officers to the park on that Saturday.

When Pastor Lee met with Tom Cho and Kim Song, the secretary of the South End Korean Merchants Association, he told them what he had learned from conversations in the community. They spoke in Korean, which was more comfortable for Song. Cho agreed that the delis that sold beer were a problem. Korean Americans had been cautioning one another for nearly a year that there was community opposition to the delis. Cho explained:

Koreans own only three of these delis in the entire South End, and our merchants association has opposed opening any additional liquor outlets. We cannot control those who sell beer, yet we are blamed for all the problems. Our Korean young people, who may understand the community better than we do, have told me that they are committed to confronting the situation. They say that we have promised something, and we should not back out now. Canceling the party would be an affront to those who are expecting gifts. And if we cancel our plans because of anonymous threats, they say this makes us vulnerable to additional threats. They say we should proceed as we had planned.

Song shook his head: "I don't understand how a gesture of kindness has led to such opposition. There is nothing political about what we are trying to do. It's not a trick. It is an open-heart gesture. We have been successful in our businesses because South End residents buy from our stores. We want to return some of the profits to them. But I do not want to create any trouble. It may be best to cancel the event. What do you think, Pastor?"

Teaching Notes

Objectives of the Case Discussion

- To begin building a listening and learning community
- To increase interest and energy for the following workshop
- To explore sources and types of case conflict
- To analyze parties and stakeholders for workshop role-plays
- To gain practice in distinguishing demands from needs and interests
- To practice developing short- and long-term goals and strategies for addressing a community conflict

Case Preparation

Create a simple discussion outline on newsprint to guide the case discussion. On one sheet, write the title "I Context: A, B, and C." On two sheets taped together, write the title "II Parties" and list the names of the parties. On a fourth sheet, write the title "III Alternatives."

The challenge for participants is to identify causes of the conflict, to understand the persons involved, and to discuss the most appropriate alternatives for Sam Lee or Tom Cho.

Reminder: The case is true, disguised, and decision-oriented. Beyond correctly stating factual information, there are no right or wrong answers.

Case Discussion

I. Context and Issues **(20 minutes)**

A. Identify the facts in the case that describe the South End community (for example, *African American residents, recently upgraded business area, wide ethnic ownership of businesses, active local business and residents association, public opposition to beer-selling delis, few delis owned by Koreans, most Korean merchants are nonresidents*).

B. Discuss the causes and contributing factors that led to the conflict between the South End Korean Merchants Association and the local residents who oppose the block party giveaway (*cultural, economic, and racial divisions; unemployment; poor communication; public anger about beer-selling delis; relatively recent arrival of Korean immigrants and their economic success; city issuance of liquor permits*).

C. Use the RIVIRS diagram in Figure 2.1 of this Leaders' Guide to assist with the analysis.

II. Parties and Stakeholders (40 minutes)
(Save a record of this discussion.)

A. Parties to the Conflict Identify each party, one at a time. List and discuss their characteristics. Block together those parties who are "undeclared," those who are in favor of the event, and those who feel the event should be canceled. *(If time is limited, discuss some but not all of the parties.)*

This can be a particularly valuable discussion within a multicultural group. If one of your goals is to build cross-cultural sensitivity and challenge stereotypes, be sure to ask participants to imagine what the specific parties may be feeling. Remember that the feelings given are not "answers" but suggestions of possible responses.

Parties	Position	Interests/Needs	Feelings
Sam Lee, *Korean pastor to many Korean merchants*	Undeclared	Concern for parishioners, community; understanding, address anger	Concerned
Tom Cho, *merchant, president of South End Korean Merchants Association*	Undeclared	Customers, community relationships, safety of businesses, keeping promises, avoiding further threats	Anxious, fearful
Joshua Taylor, *pastor of AME Church, city and community activist*	Undeclared	Concern for parishioners, community, dialogue	Concerned
Eli Johnson, *African American businessman, community activist*	Against	Ethnic pride, area youth, jobs, destructive influences (deli alcohol)	Suspicious, proud

Parties	Position	Interests/Needs	Feelings
Bill Kennedy, *president of South End Business and Residents Association*	Against	Avoid racial tension, upgraded area, cooperation, consultation	Worried, ignored
Doris Allen, *resident, community social services*	In favor	Area poverty, community needs	Upset, protective
Korean young people	In favor	Keeping promises, preventing additional threats	Determined
Captain Larkin, *local police*	Undeclared	Avoiding confrontation, maintaining harmony, appreciates Koreans, is against delis	Concerned
Kim Song, *Korean merchant*	Probably against	Thanking customers, avoiding confrontation	Anxious, uncertain

B. Stakeholders Identify individuals who could have an effect on transforming the situation but have not been identified as a party to it *(local youth, taxpayers, authors of negative flyers).*

III. Alternatives: Process, Goals, Strategies   (15–20 minutes)

Pastor Lee has spoken to many people in the community and gotten a clearer picture of the issues. Reverend Taylor has offered to assist if he is needed. Lee's goal is to move toward conflict transformation rather than having parties polarize around their positions, which could lead to open confrontation at the park.

1. What strategies should he use?

2. Identify specific strategies for meeting short-term and long-term goals that address causes of the conflict.

This section can be handled by a group role-play. The workshop facilitator can assume the role of Pastor Lee and ask the workshop participants to advise him. The discussion of goals and strategies could also be conducted in small groups. Rather than giving oral reports, each small group can post a list of either short- or long-term goals and strategies on newsprint. Workshop participants can then read the lists independently.

IV. Resources   (5 minutes)

A. What resources can Pastor Lee call on to achieve the identified goals? *(Reverend Taylor as a possible co-mediator or co-facilitator, other community residents, police)*

B. If Pastor Lee (or another person) becomes a mediator, group facilitator, or initiator of mediation in this situation, what personal skills and abilities does this person need? *(listening, patience, balanced support of parties, ability to work with others)*

V. Closing   (5 minutes)

What did you learn from your colleagues in this case discussion? *(This question is particularly helpful with a culturally diverse group of participants.)*

Role-Play #1: Paraphrasing

Facilitator Pastor Sam Lee

Parties Bill Kennedy, Tom Cho

Objectives
- To help workshop participants practice their active listening skills
- To develop ways to help parties in conflict feel safe
- To enable the parties to understand one another better

Case Update In separate conversations with Pastor Lee, Bill Kennedy and Tom Cho offered to meet to discuss their differences. They both agreed that Pastor Lee should facilitate the meeting.

(Before the role-play, set the scene for all participants, and discuss which principles Pastor Lee might follow to determine the best place for him to meet with Bill Kennedy and Tom Cho.)

Profile: Pastor Sam Lee

You believe that greater understanding between some of the parties who hold different perspectives will help the South End community from becoming further polarized. You responded to the offers by Bill Kennedy and Tom Cho to talk to one another. They both agreed to meet with you to discuss the situation.

Though they may not reach agreement about the block party, you hope to enable the two men to understand each other's concerns. While facilitating the meeting, keep the following things in mind:

1. Be clear that the meeting's goal is to reach better understanding, not resolution of any issues.

2. Your role is to facilitate their discussion, not to take sides.

3. Ask both parties to suggest and agree to some basic ground rules, such as no interruptions and brevity.

4. Get agreement on who speaks first.

5. Paraphrase and summarize their points to build trust and calm their anger or anxiety.

Profile: Bill Kennedy

You are a long-term resident of the South End and president of the South End Business and Residents Association. You are very distressed about the tension surrounding the Korean merchants. They have been in the area for about ten years. None of them have joined the association, although membership was opened to nonresident business owners five years ago. The Koreans formed their own business association and then didn't have the courtesy to notify you or the South End Association about their block party.

Most Koreans keep to themselves and never employ local youngsters who need jobs. They haven't seemed at all interested in helping the community until this turkey event surfaced. You suspect their "giveaway" is related to community anger about the Korean beer-selling delis. The Koreans should probably cancel the block party to avoid a confrontation, which would be destructive to the community and the positive image you and your association have worked so hard to develop. You appreciate that Pastor Lee sought your advice. You are willing to meet with Tom Cho because you felt that Lee heard your concerns and was genuinely interested in the community. However, you are not so sure about Cho, the president of the Korean Merchants Association.

Profile: Tom Cho

You are the owner of a small shoe store in the South End and president of the South End Korean Merchants Association. You are very concerned about the angry literature that opposes the block party the merchants have planned. You welcomed the opportunity to meet with Bill Kennedy, president of the South End Business and Residents Association. He needs to understand that you do not want to disappoint residents by canceling the party. You are afraid that if the Korean merchants give in to the unsigned flyers, the harassment will increase.

When you opened your store in the South End seven years ago, you understood that the South End Business and Residents Association was for residents only, as its name implies. You helped other Korean merchants form their own association. None of them were residents of the South End, and several of the older, respected merchants did not speak English well enough to feel comfortable in settings conducted only in English.

Pastor Lee indicated that some South End people believe that Koreans do not care about the area because their stores do not hire young African Americans. At the Korean Merchants Association meetings, you have proposed hiring local employees. This, however, continues to be a problem for some store owners, who are uneasy with local young men who come into their stores playing loud music. You know that most merchants do not hire anyone to work in their stores because most families are struggling and unable to pay for employees and benefits. It is customary for Korean children to work in family businesses without pay. This is the only way most small stores make any profit at all.

You hope Pastor Lee can help you gain Kennedy's support for the Korean merchants' initiative.

Role-Play # 2: Storytelling

Facilitator   Reverend Juanita Gonzales

Parties   Eli Johnson, Doris Allen

Objectives *(for facilitator role)*

- To practice creating a safe environment for conflicting parties
- To employ active listening and summarizing skills
- To develop a neutral list of issues
- To resolve one or more issues *(if time permits)*

Getting an agreement between Allen and Johnson will not resolve the issue in the multiparty conflict of whether or not to hold the party. However, in terms of "dividing the problems," greater understanding and possibly reaching an agreement between these two parties may have a positive impact on developing a resolution that is acceptable to all involved. Incorporate into the plenary debriefing of the role-play a discussion of next steps for the Ministerial Alliance.

Case Update

It is now two weeks before the block party sponsored by the South End Korean Merchants Association. Tension remains high in the South End. Members of the merchants' group have taken different positions on holding or canceling the event. There is also a division within the African American leadership represented by Eli Johnson, businessman and activist, who says the party should be canceled, and Doris Allen, director of the Community Assistance Program, who supports the distribution of needed resources.

South End religious leaders appealed to the Ministerial Alliance for assistance. Alliance members Pastor Sam Lee and Rev. Joshua Taylor propose that Johnson and Allen meet with a third party who is unrelated to either the African American or the Korean communities. They identified Rev. Juanita Gonzales, pastor of a multicultural church in the South End, who chairs the Ministerial Alliance Task Force on Cross-Cultural Communications. She is respected by both Johnson and Allen, who have worked with her on issues of human rights.

Profile: Juanita Gonzales

Local ministers Sam Lee and Joshua Taylor have asked you to help reduce tension between two South End community leaders so that resolution concerning the block party crisis might be reached in the next few days. You admire both Doris Allen and Eli Johnson, who are respected community leaders. Both have pride in being African American. Johnson has been openly opposed to the block party, and Allen has made equally strong statements about a unique opportunity to meet community needs. Each party agreed to meet the other—with you as facilitator—to hear things out. Although you may not get agreement about the block party in this brief meeting, you hope to enable Allen and Johnson to express their feelings, to communicate better, and to identify the issues that divide them. While facilitating the meeting, consider the following approach:

Introduction

1. Explain the process and goals for the discussion.

2. Clarify your role as facilitator.

3. Get agreement on some basic ground rules such as respect and not interrupting each other.

4. Get agreement on who speaks first.

Storytelling

1. Have the parties share their perspectives and primary concerns, first one party and then the other.

2. Ignore their stated positions and use open questions or statements and paraphrasing to help them identify their underlying needs and interests.

3. Listen for and identify common concerns and specific areas of disagreement.

4. Together, create a list of specific issues to focus on in further discussions. *(Continue with the role-play if you feel you can help the parties address one of the issues.)*

Profile: Eli Johnson

You are suspicious of the motives of the South End Korean Merchants Association. Their "block party" looks more like a buyoff of African American customers to distract them from protesting the Korean-owned delis that sell beer. All these delis, no matter who owns them, should be boycotted as a source of corruption.

You are also upset that the Koreans did not acknowledge in their giveaway announcement the name change for Malcolm X Park. You are not surprised by this since the Korean merchants don't live in the community and are not really connected with the issues of the South End. Doris Allen is a good woman, and you are amazed that she does not see the affront this turkey buyoff is to African American dignity. You know some brothers are hungry, but this is too high a price to pay for being stuffed with turkey. The young people need the kind of self-respect that comes from a good job, not a handout.

You don't know who printed those negative flyers, but if the offensive block party goes on as scheduled, you are committed to gathering a group to join the protest march. You would, however, prefer to find a way to avoid an open confrontation in which everyone might lose.

Juanita Gonzales, who asked you to meet with Allen, is a sharp lady for whom you have deep respect. Maybe Rev. Gonzales can help Allen understand that this party would hinder—not help—residents in the South End.

Profile: Doris Allen

You have just begun to get the Community Assistance Program, which helps area residents who are in desperate need, off the ground. The Korean merchants, who admittedly do a good business in the neighborhood, decide to say "Happy Thanksgiving" with gifts of essentials such as food and clothing. You don't want to speculate about the motives of the donors. You want help for the people.

You are aware that residents like Eli Johnson think the Korean merchants are not connected to the community. But they are connected enough to know that there are hungry people out there without warm clothes for the winter. Sure, it may be good for their business, but the party may also be their way of saying thank you. In addition, this kind of event just might encourage other merchants to support the community by contributing essential goods for the poor.

And what's so bad about the Koreans missing the name change of Malcolm X Park? So did a lot of the black residents of the South End. The older Koreans probably don't even know who Malcolm X was.

If the protest continues, there could be confrontations between some residents and Korean merchants as well as between residents who want to stop the party and those who want it to continue. If Capt. Larkin and his police force have to intervene, the residents suffer, and the publicity hurts all of the merchants too.

You believe that Eli Johnson is a fine businessman and a committed activist and that he could stop the protest movement if he wanted to. But his pride has blinded him to the needs of the community. However, Rev. Gonzalez is a good pastor, and she knows how to help people talk to one another. She ought to be able to get Johnson straightened out!

Role-Play #3: A Multiparty Meeting

For a large group, a fishbowl approach works well with this role-play. Prepare large name tags for the eight principal parties, and have a newsprint easel and markers available for the facilitators. Divide the participants into four small groups, by either assigning the groups or having the participants select their roles (meeting facilitators, South End Business and Residents Association, Community Assistance Program, or South End Korean Merchants Association). Have copies of the appropriate role available for all participants in each group. *(Refer to the basic workshop, Day Two, Section XVII.B., "Multiparty Facilitation Role-Play," for detailed suggestions about conducting and debriefing this role-play.)*

Alert participants that it is not realistic to assume that the parties have authority to make decisions for their organizations or that conflicts will be resolved in the time available.

Facilitators   Trusted community leaders

Parties   *South End Business and Residents Association:* Bill Kennedy and Eli Johnson
Community Assistance Program: Doris Allen and Maria Hernandez
South End Korean Merchants Association: Tom Cho and Paul Chee

Objectives *(for participants)*

- To apply what was learned in the workshop
- To experience the potential and challenges of a multiparty facilitation

Case Update   The block party is one week away, and the South End is tense. Some groups are threatening a protest march while others want the gift giving to continue as planned. The parties have not resolved their differences. The community is confused, anxious, and unsure of what to expect.

Through the intervention of Rev. Taylor and Pastor Lee, spokespersons for some of the parties have agreed to meet with two trusted community leaders to discuss their differences. Lee and Taylor have spoken to representatives of three groups and understand their public positions to be as follows. *(Post these positions on the board or on newsprint.)*

> *South End Business and Residents Association* (represented by Bill Kennedy and Eli Johnson): Members continue to see the block party as an attempt by the Koreans to exploit and manipulate poor people. They demand that the block party be canceled.

Community Assistance Program (represented by Doris Allen and Maria Hernandez, a local social service provider): Social service providers and many poor families are convinced that canceling the block party would jeopardize the possibility of feeding and clothing persons in need. They urge that the block party be held.

South End Korean Merchants Association (represented by Tom Cho and Paul Chee, a younger member of the Korean community): The majority of members believe that canceling the party would disappoint the community and invite more threats. They are committed to holding the party as planned.

Profile: Two Trusted Community Leaders

You are one of the co-facilitators of a meeting between representatives of the (1) South End Business and Residents Association, (2) the Community Assistance Program, and (3) the South End Korean Merchants Association. You are a trusted leader in the community who is experienced in group facilitation. You have spoken to all of the parties, and they have agreed to meet with you to discuss their differences.

As a co-facilitator, you want to be clear that you will not make any decisions for the group. You are there to facilitate their conversation, to build understanding, and to seek a range of mutually agreeable options. You want to look for ways to strengthen the parties' relationships and empower them to address some of the "causal and contributing factors" that surfaced during the case analysis.

Things to Decide in Advance

- The room arrangement

- Your opening comments (including any ground rules)

- The order in which one member of each team presents a two-minute introductory statement

Your Strategies

- To help the parties listen to one another by paraphrasing their concerns

- To help the group identify common ground and the most critical issues that need to be addressed

- To post the issues and select one to discuss

- To progress as far as possible in the time allotted

Profile: Doris Allen

You are the director of the Community Assistance Program. You have had visits from many poor community members who are concerned about the threat to cancel the block party being organized by the Korean merchants. Most of them are struggling to make ends meet. They have all looked forward to the food and clothing offered at this party.

You understand Eli Johnson's concern about the lack of interaction between the Korean merchants and the local residents, and you strongly support the call to stop the selling of cheap liquor. However, you are not sure the South End Korean Merchants Association has the power to intervene. You believe the Koreans are genuine in wanting to show their gratitude for the community support. The event may not only be an opportunity to start building relationships with the Korean community, but it could also become a model for other merchants to assume some responsibility for residents in need. But you are unsure about the level of opposition to the party, and you want at all costs to avoid a violent confrontation. You and Maria Hernandez, your co-worker, must remember that your primary concern is the ongoing struggle to feed poor families. Your program needs all the help it can get to provide for these families. Your public position is that you cannot afford to have this party canceled. You and Marcia agreed to prepare a two-minute opening statement that Marcia will give at the meeting.

Profile: Bill Kennedy

You are the president of the South End Business and Residents Association. A number of community members have approached you to express their concerns about the block party being organized by the Korean merchants. They are convinced that this is a plot by the Koreans to manipulate and exploit their community and move attention away from the Korean delis that sell cheap liquor to South End young people. They say that the Koreans are only interested in personal enrichment and that the young people need jobs, not alcohol. Agreeing to support the block party would not challenge the Koreans to show a real interest in the community.

Personally, you support Doris Allen and Maria Hernandez in their work and understand the need of the Community Assistance Program for sufficient funds and resources to feed low-income and poor families. It just might be possible to work out a way to hold the party. Although you still don't know who sent out the negative flyers, you and the other merchants might be able to discredit the protest movement if you had sufficient reasons. The last thing the community needs is a violent confrontation.

You are convinced that without your intervention, however, there is enough support from the community to cancel the party. You want the Korean merchants to stop selling cheap liquor and to commit themselves to cooperate more with the South End Business and Residents Association. Your public position is that the block party must be canceled.

You've been invited to join in the multiparty community facilitation to find a solution to this difficult situation. You know Eli Johnson well as a businessperson, and you know his passion for and involvement in the community. He agreed to join you in this meeting to represent your position. One of you will develop a two-minute opening statement for the meeting.

Profile: Tom Cho

You are the president of the South End Korean Merchants Association. A number of Korean young people expressed strong opinions about holding the block party. They maintain that it is unacceptable to make public promises without delivering on them. People are expecting a gift, and it would be unfair to those who really need the food if you were to cancel the party. Other members of the association say that canceling the party shows you are afraid, which could subject them to even more harassment.

Privately, you understand Bill Kennedy's concern about the lack of interaction between the South End Korean Merchants Association and the South End Business and Residents Association. You are willing to initiate ideas with your business associates for new ways to cooperate with residents and other local merchants. But they need to understand that you had genuinely hoped that the party would show your gratitude for the residents' support of your stores.

Although you are deeply concerned about the possibility of a violent confrontation, which would be destructive to the whole community, your public position continues to be that the Korean merchants must keep their promises and hold the block party.

Paul Chee, a young Korean American who speaks English fluently, will join you in the multiparty facilitation. You agreed to prepare a two-minute opening statement for the meeting.

LORD OF THE DANCE

Case Study

Al Bannon, moderator of the congregation for Center Church, stood before a regular meeting of the congregation and again called the members to order. A few people had begun to speak out of turn, and two older members of the congregation appeared to be leaving before the meeting was over. Again, he asked the members of the congregation for their specific suggestions to address the issue before them—how best to resolve the dispute over Hymn 261.

Center Church had been located in this urban area for many years and drew members from several miles away. However, in the past few years, membership had begun to dwindle as fewer young families joined the church. In an attempt to minister to the neighborhood near the church and to draw in younger members, the church had hired a youth director two years ago. Sarah Reynolds developed an exciting youth program. There were now more than thirty members of the church's teenage youth group.

Several months ago, the young people raised funds to purchase copies of a new hymnal, "Sing and Rejoice," for the congregation to use along with the regular hymnal. At least once a month, the pastor tried to use contemporary hymns from this book in worship. Four weeks ago, an older member of the congregation, who remained unnamed, protested to the board of deacons that Hymn 261, "Lord of the Dance," was inappropriate because it was disrespectful, promoted dancing, and referred to Jesus "with the devil on his back." After studying the hymn and discussing the situation, the deacons, all of whom were older members of the congregation, wrote a letter to the youth group suggesting three choices:

1. Tear out the page of the offending hymn from each hymnal.

2. Paste the two pages of Hymn 261 together.

3. Withdraw the hymnal from congregational use.

Most members of the congregation were unaware of the situation until they arrived at church two weeks later and discovered the following message stamped on page 261 of the new hymnal: "We consider this song to be unworthy of our Lord. Board of Deacons."

At the congregational meeting, the main topic of discussion was the recent action of the board of deacons. Al Bannon, who moderated the meeting, felt that the church seemed about evenly split on the propriety of the

---

This case study is adapted from a role-play by Robert Kreider from *The Role-Play Book* (Akron, Pa.: Mennonite Conciliation Service, 1997) and was originally published as a case study in *When Good People Quarrel* by Robert Kreider and Rachel Waltner Goossen (Scottdale, Pa.: Herald Press, 1989). Used and adapted by permission.

deacon's action. Mr. Warren, chair of the board of deacons, stated at the congregational meeting that the deacons decided to act because they had not received any response from the youth group. The youth leader, Sarah Reynolds, responded that the group had met only once since receiving the demanding letter and had not yet come to a consensus on how best to respond.

Some members of the congregation expressed concern about the theology of a hymn that depicted Jesus dancing with the devil on his back. One of the deacons declared, "Our theologians at the seminary would be highly distressed that we are teaching such irreverence to our young people." A leader of the adult Sunday school class countered, "Some theologians would be pleased that our young people see Jesus as relevant to their lives." One of the seven members of the youth group who had joined the church, David Lee, reminded the congregation that the pastor had read from scripture only last Sunday about David dancing in front of the ark. After some younger church members expressed very strong feelings about "defacing our songbook," three of the twelve deacons announced their resignation from the board.

Al Bannon was concerned that the songbook controversy had opened long-festering antagonisms between older members of the congregation and the young people, especially the youth from poor families living near the church. The theological differences that were being raised could also lead to further division. Bannon was a respected member of the congregation and had served effectively as moderator for three years. The pastor had been in the congregation for only six months. He and Bannon had quietly conferred during the meeting and agreed that Bannon should try to initiate some plan toward resolution before the meeting ended. Bannon did not have strong feelings about the song in question. His primary concern at this point was to develop a process that would let the deacons and the youth group resolve their differences.

Teaching Notes

Objectives of the Case Discussion

- To analyze how the setting, history, and parties in the case study influenced the conflict
- To sharpen the participants' ability to empathize with various perspectives
- To practice differentiating demands (position) from interests and needs
- To sharpen skills for developing short- and long-term goals and strategies
- To increase interest and energy in the topic and the workshop
- To develop a base for role-plays and skills practice

Case Discussion

I. Context and Issues   (20 minutes)

A. Describe the setting of the case (for example, *urban congregation, poverty in the surrounding area, new youth leader, growing youth group, purchase of new hymnbook by youth*).

B. Discuss the implied or suspected causes and contributing factors that led to the confrontation over the hymnbook (*congregational and community change, a woman in leadership, theological differences, social differences*).

C. After listing several factors on the board, use the RIVIRS diagram in Figure 2.1 of this Leaders' Guide to assist with the analysis. Consider how issues in each of the RIVIRS categories may need to be handled differently to reach a sustainable agreement that can help lead to healing in the congregation.

II. Parties and Stakeholders   (20 minutes)
(Save a record of this discussion.)

A. Al Bannon Who is he? What is his role? What is he most concerned about?

B. Parties to the Conflict Make a chart with columns with the headings shown here. Identify each party, one at a time, and list and discuss their characteristics.

Person	Position on Whether Deacons' Actions Were Justified	Interests/ Needs	Feelings
Sarah Reynolds, *youth leader*			
The Pastor			
Mr. Warren, *spokesperson for the deacons*			
David Lee, *spokesperson for the youth group*			
Leader of the adult class			

If time is limited, develop Bannon, Reynolds, Warren, and Lee sufficiently to conduct the role-play in which Bannon facilitates a meeting with three parties.

III. Alternatives: Process, Goals, Strategies   (20 minutes)

Al Bannon is facing a serious congregational conflict. If his goal is to move toward constructive conflict transformation rather than push the parties further into polarized positions on the action of the deacons, he must determine what strategies would be effective.

Distinguish between strategies that could meet his short-term goal of dealing with the immediate conflict and those for long-term goals such as better relationships among members. Consider the following questions:

1. What principles provide a foundation for the goals and strategies suggested?

2. What is the most effective sequence of strategies?

3. Who should be involved in the decision about the deacons' actions?

4. Who should be involved in developing long-term strategies for the congregation?

Refer to the identified causes of the conflict. What approaches could help the congregation use the present conflict as an opportunity to heal some of its divisions and bring about constructive changes that would lead to greater harmony?

IV. Resources   **(15 minutes)**

What resources can Al Bannon call on to achieve the identified goals?

V. Local Application *(optional)*   **(15 minutes or more)**

In a plenary discussion or small groups, apply learning from the case study to developing guidelines for dealing with congregational conflict.

Role-Play: Introduction and Storytelling

(This case has only one printed role-play. We suggest you use it after you have introduced the first two stages of mediation. Depending on the time available, this role-play enables the facilitator to stop after the Introduction and Storytelling Stages or to continue and practice all four stages of the mediation process. This role-play works well with co-facilitators.)

Facilitator   Al Bannon

Parties   Mr. Warren, Sarah Reynolds, David Lee

Preintervention   Before entering this role-play, set up "spot role-plays" in plenary session. Have different participants assume the role of Al Bannon, urging either Mr. Warren or Sarah Reynolds to attend the meeting.

- Discuss which approaches work best in encouraging people to meet with an adversary.

- What discourages them?

- What issues should Al Bannon discuss in these conversations?

Following the Role-Play

In the discussion following the role-play, ask each group:

- How could the meeting between representatives of the deacons and the youth group ultimately have a positive effect on the whole congregation?

- What concrete steps could each person directly involved in the dispute take toward healing divisions in the congregation?

- Which moral, cultural, and spiritual resources could help the people involved in the conflict?

Case Update   Mr. Warren, representing the deacons, and Sarah Reynolds, the youth leader, agreed to meet at the church with Al Bannon on the day after the congregational meeting to discuss the situation regarding the contemporary hymnbooks. Sarah Reynolds urged that a member of the youth group, David Lee, be allowed to attend the session and speak for the young people. Warren reluctantly agreed to this addition.

This role-play was adapted from a role-play titled "The Deacons and the Youth Group" by Robert Kreider from *The Role-Play Book* (Akron, Pa.: Mennonite Conciliation Service, 1997) and was originally published as a case study in the book *When Good People Quarrel* by Robert Kreider and Rachel Waltner Goossen (Scottdale, Pa.: Herald Press, 1989). Used by permission.

Profile: Al Bannon

You are the moderator of the congregation. Your primary objectives in the meeting are to give an opportunity for the parties to state their views and to encourage each party to listen respectfully to the others. To accomplish this, you want to help them feel comfortable in the meeting. You spoke with all three by telephone last night. While facilitating the meeting, consider the following approach:

Introduction

1. Welcome the parties, and explain the process and goals for the meeting.

2. Clarify your role.

3. Get agreement about some ground rules, such as not interrupting one another, and decide who speaks first.

Storytelling

1. Use positive paraphrasing to build trust and calm their anger or anxiety.

2. Rather than focus on declared positions, use open questions or statements to help the parties identify their underlying interests and primary concerns.

3. When the parties are comfortable, "release" them to speak to one another. Look for *their* suggestions.

You would feel some real progress if you could help them gain greater understanding of each other's position, identify the issues that divide them, and begin to identify ways of resolving one of these issues such that it would be acceptable to both the deacons and the youth group.

Profile: Mr. Warren

You are the chairman of the board of deacons. You are deeply concerned about the drift toward worldly values that you sense among young people, especially the poor neighborhood youth who enjoy the benefits of the church but have not been willing to commit to membership. You have tried to be both patient and flexible about their noise and the wear-and-tear on the room where they meet, but the last straw came when the song "Lord of the Dance" was sung in church. When a respected older member of the congregation also complained about this song, you gently raised the issue with the youth group. The options you gave them to deal with the problem appeared reasonable to the deacons and reflected your opinion that the majority of the hymns in the book are fine and can be used.

When the youth group did not have the courtesy of responding to your concerns, you reluctantly decided to stamp the message in the songbook out of genuine concern for the church. The entire congregation has overreacted! In a recent sermon, the new pastor took the side of the young people by citing positive Scripture references to dancing, and a number of people attacked your actions and even your motives. You are willing to explain your motivation to the youth group leader, but you do not consider that any apologies to the young people are in order.

Profile: Sarah Reynolds

You are the leader of the youth group. You support the young people and feel they should be able to speak for themselves in the meeting with Al Bannon and Mr. Warren, chair of the board of deacons. You agreed to attend the meeting only to support David Lee, the president of the youth group. You plan to speak only if David is unfairly attacked.

Profile: David Lee

You are the president of the Center Church youth group. You and the other young people were surprised and angered by the action of the board of deacons. "Lord of the Dance" is a harmless, joyful song. It is hard to believe that anyone could object to it. What upsets you most is the manner in which the deacons acted. Their response appears to you as underhanded and manipulative. The youth group was seriously considering the options presented to them by the deacons, but there was only one meeting of the group between the day Sarah Reynolds received the notice and the defacing of the hymnbooks you had worked so hard to purchase. Members of the youth group did not mean any disrespect; they needed more time to give a thoughtful response.

You also suspect that the deacons really don't want the youth in the church, and you are afraid that some of the more hesitant, unchurched young people that you and Sarah Reynolds have worked so hard to welcome will now leave the group. The only way to begin to heal the hurt and alienation of the youth group would be an apology by the deacons and a rescinding of their actions.

CHAPTER 8

Independent Role-Plays

NEIGHBORHOOD CONFLICT: CHILDREN AND DOGS

Profile: Neighbor East

You are sixty-five years old. You live by yourself in a neighborhood with a lot of crime. You have two dogs that live with you. They give you security, and they are your friends. They are nice dogs, and they cause no problems.

However, your neighbor has two boys who are causing big problems! They are little brats who throw stones on your roof and tease your dogs. They throw stones at the dogs and walk along your fence with sticks, poking at the dogs. Of course the dogs bark and growl, and because your fence has some loose boards, the dogs sometimes get out and run after the boys. Then the boys go running into their house, and the parents complain about your vicious dogs. *You want your neighbors to make their boys behave.* Recently you agreed to have another neighbor, whom you know and respect, assist in resolving this problem. You are now meeting in this neighbor's house.

The role-plays in this chapter were adapted from original role-plays written by Ronald S. Kraybill.

Profile: Neighbor West

You are the parent of two boys, aged six and nine. They are nice boys and cause you no problems. But your neighbor is a big problem! This person has two large, vicious dogs that are a real threat to the neighborhood. Your sons are terrified of them. The dogs bark and growl every time your boys go past the house. Worse, about once a week, the dogs get out through holes in the fence that your neighbor is too stubborn to fix. The dogs have chased your boys on several occasions, and you are really worried that one of your sons is going to be badly bitten. *The dogs must go!* Recently, you agreed to have another neighbor, whom you know and respect, assist in resolving this problem. You are now meeting in this neighbor's house.

Profile: Neighbor North (mediator)

Your neighbors have been having an argument for several months about dogs and kids. You don't know exactly what is going on, but you decided to offer to help. You are not only concerned about their relationship but also that other people in the neighborhood may start taking sides, and the problem could get even worse. You are friends with both neighbors, and you asked them to come to your house to talk about the situation. They both agreed, saying that they trust your judgment. Your goals are to help them feel "safe," to help them understand each other better, and to empower them to come to mutually agreeable resolutions about the issues that divide them.

A Few Suggestions

- Help the parties feel welcome; affirm their good intentions; clarify the goals of the meeting and your role (that you will not take sides and that they will make the decisions).

- Get agreement on any ground rules or guidelines.

- Decide who speaks first.

- As each person tells his or her story, use positive paraphrasing to build trust and calm anger or anxiety.

- Use open questions or statements to help them recognize their underlying needs and interests.

- Identify any common ground. Identify and get agreement on the issues (in nonjudgmental terms). Choose one issue at a time. Brainstorm options for resolution, and work out the most acceptable option or options. Develop a clear agreement on specific steps for resolving each issue.

THE STUDENT AND THE JAZZ MUSICIAN

Profile: Neighbor East, Student

You are a community college student and help support your family by working in a bakery. Your classes are in the afternoon, so you need to study in the evening. You have to get up every morning at 5:00 A.M. to go to work at the bakery. You have moved into a new apartment building, and your next-door neighbor is a jazz musician who has no consideration for others. This neighbor plays music loudly three or four nights a week, alone or with friends. Your neighbor leaves doors and windows wide open and always plays the music at top volume. You have asked this person several times to keep the volume down, and each time he or she reacts angrily and refuses to do anything. Your mother works a night shift, so the noise doesn't bother her, but she knows the building manager, and you may be able to apply some pressure because this tenant is clearly violating the apartment regulations. Your position is, "If you don't turn down the volume, I'll get you evicted!"

Profile: Neighbor West, Jazz Musician

You are a jazz musician and make your living on your music. This requires you to practice on a regular basis, alone and with your band. You often practice in your first-floor apartment, and people in the neighborhood and the building seem to enjoy the music. Sometimes you see people bopping and dancing as they pass while you practice. But the young person who just moved in next door has been a real hassle, constantly telling you that your music is terrible and loud.

If your music is really disturbing anyone, you are willing to keep it down. But nobody else has complained. If someone does have problems, the person should come to you like a decent human being and not insult you. This punk just has a chip on the shoulder, and you resent that this brat is giving you a hard time. Your position is, "I was here first. Nobody else is complaining. If you don't like my music, that's tough."

Profile: Concerned Neighbor (mediator)

Your neighbors have an ongoing feud about noise, and you are worried that it may come to blows. You understand that the student's position is "If you don't turn down the volume, I'll get you evicted!" and that the musician's is "I was here first. Nobody else is complaining. If you don't like my music, that's tough."

The two have agreed to meet in your apartment to try to sort things out.

A Few Suggestions

- Make it clear that it is up to them to decide what they want to do; you will not take sides.

- Help them feel comfortable and safe at the meeting so that ultimately they will be able to talk to each other and come to an agreement they will both be able and willing to keep.

- Begin by clarifying your role, describing the process, and establishing some ground rules.

- To help each party *understand* the other, have each one tell his or her side of the story. Paraphrase when necessary. After each one speaks, *summarize* the concerns expressed in a way that focuses on the person's needs and interests, not the positions the person has taken. Recognize the concerns the two of them have in common.

- Get agreement on the specific *issues* or problems on which they need to focus.

- Choose one issue, reenter discussion, and brainstorm options. Try to reach agreement on one issue.

CHAPTER 9

Sacred Text Studies

THE FOLLOWING TOPICS and passages are drawn from the Christian New Testament, Hebrew Scriptures, the Muslim Qur'an, and a civic document holding moral authority. All of these passages have been prayerfully studied in multifaith gatherings. Chapter Three offers workshop leaders specific suggestions for enabling participants to encounter and learn from these texts.

 Additional sample questions on biblical texts with specific references to the workshop designs can be found on the Jossey-Bass Web site, www.josseybass.com/peaceskills.

SACRED TEXT STUDY #1

Recognition and Listening—Mark 10:46–52

Workshop Design

This study is particularly applicable to the basic workshop Day One section on introduction to paraphrasing.

Time

60-90 minutes

Text

> And they came to Jericho; and as he was leaving Jericho with his disciples and a great multitude, Bartimaeus, a blind beggar, the son of Timaeus, was sitting by the roadside. And when he heard that it was Jesus of Nazareth, he began to cry out and say, "Jesus, Son of David, have mercy on me!" And many rebuked him, telling him to

be silent; but he cried out all the more, "Son of David, have mercy on me!" And Jesus stopped and said, "Call him." And they called the blind man, saying to him, "Take heart; rise, he is calling you." And throwing off his mantle he sprang up and came to Jesus. And Jesus said to him, "What do you want me to do for you?" And the blind man said to him, "Master, let me receive my sight." And Jesus said to him, "Go your way; your faith has made you well." And immediately he received his sight and followed him on the way. (Revised Standard Version)

Sample Questions[1]

Begin by centering and by reading the text aloud, or have members of the group read it aloud.

This scripture study can be introduced by a role-play if participants can imagine themselves part of a great crowd leaving Jericho and heading toward Jerusalem. People sometimes feel less self-conscious and more focused on experiencing the interactions of the role-play if they keep their eyes shut. As the narrator, lead them through this human drama:

Be the crowd waiting. Express your feelings by speaking aloud.

Be the blind Bartimaeus calling to Jesus. What are you saying? Feeling?

Be the crowd after Jesus has recognized Bartimaeus. How do you respond?

Be Bartimaeus as Jesus calls you to him. How do you feel?

Be Bartimaeus as Jesus asks, "What do you want me to do for you?" and listens for your reply.

Regather the group, and pose the following questions, leaving time between them for thoughtful responses.

1. Who is Bartimaeus? What is the status of a beggar?

2. What might Bartimaeus have heard about this Jesus? Teacher, listener, prophet, healer, king? Do you think Bartimaeus expected to be recognized by Jesus? Why and how? What is it about us that we desperately need to be recognized and honored?

3. How might the authorities hear the title "Son of David"? What was ahead of Jesus at Jerusalem? Why do the crowds and perhaps even the disciples attempt to silence Bartimaeus?

4. How does Jesus respond to this rebuke of Bartimaeus? Why and how does Jesus recognize Bartimaeus?

5. How do you understand the change in the response of those who tried to silence Bartimaeus? What is the crowd's relationship to Jesus and now to Bartimaeus? What does this tell us about crowd mentality and intervention in community conflicts?

6. What happens to Bartimaeus when Jesus recognizes and calls him? Why doesn't Jesus go to Bartimaeus, who can't see? Why does Jesus direct others to call Bartimaeus? What is the meaning of a beggar's throwing off his mantle? By leaving it behind, what is he saying?

7. What has empowered Bartimaeus to cry out, leap up, and present himself before Jesus to ask for his life as a blind beggar to be transformed?

8. Why does Jesus ask him what he wants? Jesus can see that Bartimaeus is blind. What will happen to Bartimaeus if he receives his sight? How do we sometimes cling to problems that keep us from being empowered? What does it take to be ready to be made whole, to be healed? What is Jesus listening for as one called the "Prince of Peace"?

9. What does it mean for Bartimaeus to "receive his sight"? Do people have different ways of seeing? Of being empowered? Of being transformed?

10. When his sight is granted, what does Jesus tell Bartimaeus to do? What does it mean to "go your way"? How do we sometimes want to control those who have been liberated? What does it mean for Bartimaeus to follow Jesus "on the way"?

11. What does this process of recognizing, listening, empowering, and liberating mean for mediators and peacebuilders?

Application to Life

Give the following instructions to participants, giving them time to respond between requests.

1. Write on a sheet of paper the name of a person or a group that you care about and who needs to be empowered or healed.

2. Write out what you want to do for that person or group.

3. Imagine they are Bartimaeus. Listen to them. Write out briefly what they might want or need that goes beyond your original assumptions.

4. How can you listen better to other people? How can you let them know you heard and understood them?

5. Ask yourself if you are willing to pay the price to respond to the needs they identify. Record what it might cost you, and indicate your reply.

6. Write either a prayer or a promise (with all the gusto and brass of a Bartimaeus) asking God or friends for help in listening to others deeply,

recognizing their humanity, and meeting their needs in ways that empower them.

Invite those who wish to share their prayers or promises to do so. Encourage people to keep a copy of their prayer or promise and be regularly reminded of it.

If you have used this study in connection with the art of listening and the skill of paraphrasing, the following words by Dietrich Bonhoeffer (1954, pp. 97–99) provide a bridge to return to the workshop.

> *The first service that one owes to others in the fellowship consists in listening to them. Just as love to God begins with listening to His Word, so the beginning of love for our brothers and sisters is learning to listen to them. Christians, especially ministers, so often think they must always contribute something when they are in the company of others. They forget that listening can be a greater service than speaking. Many people are looking for an ear that will listen. They do not find it among Christians, because these Christians are talking where they should be listening. But the person who can no longer listen to others will soon be no longer listening to God either. This is the beginning of the death of the spiritual life, and in the end, there is nothing left but spiritual chatter and clerical condescension arrayed in pious works. Christians have forgotten that the ministry of listening has been committed to them by the One who is the great listener and whose work they should share. We should listen with the ears of God that we may speak the Word of God.*

Background on the Questions

1. Bartimaeus means "Son of Timaeus." He is so low on the social ladder that he does not have a name of his own.

2. "Son of David" was a title that implied a king or potential ruler of Israel and a threat to Roman rule. Rumors about Jesus that could have reached Jericho included that he was a wise teacher, a prophet who knew the future, a healer and miracle worker, and even the Messiah who would save Israel.

3. Jesus and the disciples were traveling to Jerusalem for the Passover festival. It was during that festival that Jesus would be arrested, accused of seeking to become "king of the Jews," and crucified by the Roman authorities.

4. A beggar's traditional request for alms was "have mercy on me." The beggar's mantle was a storage place for coins, provided shelter, and might have been his only principal possession.

SACRED TEXT STUDY #2

Healing and Reconciliation—Genesis 25–33

Workshop Design

This sacred text, presented as a drama, was designed to help participants consider various sources of conflict and discover elements in traditional ways of dealing with conflict that offer insights into the process of healing, forgiveness, and reconciliation.[2] It is also an excellent study to use with a discussion of the *Peace Skills* Manual, Chapter Ten, "Moving Toward Reconciliation." The study raises the importance of the spiritual dimension of healing. The goal of the study is to encourage serious reflection about reconciliation rather than to provide answers.

Time

60–90 minutes

Text

The selected passages from Genesis 25–33 (Hebrew Torah and Christian Old Testament) are cited throughout the following study. They come from the story of Jacob and Esau, twin sons of Isaac, who was the son of Abraham. In contrast with the other scripture studies, the text covers several chapters in the Book of Genesis. The questions for discussion focus on the sections of this long story that apply specifically to the relationship between the two brothers.

Introducing the Scripture and Sample Questions

Rather than read the selected passages aloud, it is much more engaging to invite four participants representing Isaac, Rebekah, Jacob, and Esau to stand in front of the group. As you *tell* the story, have the relevant characters come forward. Ask them to reflect on their feelings or perspectives at different points in the story before you turn to the full group for reflections.

For your own preparation, study the passages in Genesis as annotated here until you are very familiar with the story. Note that there are slight variations between the verse numbers in the Torah and Christian Old Testament. This is an exciting story that can be told with energy and action.

Genesis 25:19–34 Set the scene with Isaac and Rebekah, who wait twenty years for children. When she finally becomes pregnant with twins, Rebekah has difficulty as the babies "jostle each other." God answers her questioning by explaining that two nations struggle within her and that the "older will serve the younger." Bring Jacob and Esau forward, showing Esau as "red and hairy" and Jacob grasping Esau's heel.

Place Esau with Isaac, Jacob with Rebekah. Describe how each relates to only one parent. Recall that Esau's birthright, as the eldest son, means he will receive the largest share of inheritance from his father. Have Jacob and Esau walk through your telling of the story of Esau selling his birthright for food.

Stop the story. Ask Esau and Jacob how they feel about what happened. Ask Isaac and Rebekah their reactions.

Genesis 27:1–41 Move forward several years. The next encounter between Esau and Jacob takes place when Isaac is very old and can no longer see. He is near death and wants to give his blessing to his favorite son. Set the scene with Isaac's instructions to Esau. Show Rebekah listening to the conversation. She goes to Jacob and tells him what she overheard. Either summarize or ask Rebekah to read verses 6–10. Tell about Jacob's initial reaction and how Rebekah cooks the meal, covers Jacob's arms with goatskins, and dresses him in Esau's clothes.

Walk through the suspenseful steps of Jacob's convincing his father that he is Esau, having Isaac touch and even smell Jacob, then eat the game. Note that when Isaac finally gives his blessing, he asks that God will make his son wealthy and powerful and that his brothers will bow down to him.

Immediately after Jacob leaves, Esau comes in for his blessing. Describe Esau's encounter with his father and his pleading for an additional blessing, which is refused. Esau cries. His father responds that Esau will live by the sword and will serve his brother but will one day throw Jacob's yoke from his neck. Esau declares that after his father dies, he will kill his brother Jacob.

Stop the story. Ask the four characters how they are feeling. Open the dialogue up to members of the group. What questions do they have of the characters? What cultural and social factors contributed to the conflict between Esau and Jacob? What systemic inequalities might be involved? How did relationships affect the conflict?

In terms of intervention in a conflict, when and how do peacemakers raise the issue of injustice? Is it possible to deal with reconciliation when one party is as angry as Esau is?

Genesis 27:42–45; 28:10–15 With Rebekah's urging, Jacob runs away to stay with Laban, his mother's brother. On the way, he dreams that God will guard him, bless him, and bring him back home again. Note that the next few chapters in the story are told only from the perspective of Jacob; there is no mention of Esau. (*At this point in the story, "Isaac" and "Rebekah" could sit down.*)

Genesis 29:1–28 Jacob falls in love with Laban's daughter Rachel and works for Laban for seven years to marry her. Laban tricks Jacob on his wedding night and substitutes Rachel's older sister, Leah. Jacob works another seven years to marry Rachel.

Genesis 30:25–26; 31:17–18 During the next six years, Jacob works for his own flocks of sheep, goats, and other animals. Although Jacob feels that Laban has taken advantage of him, he has become wealthy and the father of many children. He decides to return home. This means he will have to face Esau.

Stop the story. Remind the group that Jacob had fled his homeland in fear of his brother, who vowed to kill him. Ask, "Why does Jacob want to return home?" "What enables people to turn and face an enemy?"

Genesis 32–33 (selected verses) Trace the remarkable steps in Jacob's journey home.

Genesis 32:4–13 (Torah), Genesis 32:3–12 (Christian Old Testament): Jacob is traveling with his two wives, his children, servants, and many animals. He first sends messengers ahead to tell Esau that he is returning home. The messengers return with news that Esau is coming to meet him with "four hundred men"—a formidable army. In fear, Jacob divides his people and flocks into two groups, hoping that if Esau attacks one, Jacob will be able to save the other.

Genesis 32:14–22 (Torah), Genesis 32:13–21 (Christian Old Testament): Jacob then decides to send his servants ahead in three separate groups, each herding many animals and following one another at some distance. He instructs each group of servants to tell Esau that the animals belong to Jacob, who is coming behind them, and that the animals are all gifts for Esau.

Genesis 32:23–30 (Torah), Genesis 32:22–29 (Christian Old Testament): The night before Jacob is to meet his brother, he sends his wives, children, and remaining possessions to the other side of a river. Jacob is all alone. The text says Jacob wrestles all night with "a man." Jacob will not let the man go until he blesses him. The "man" changes Jacob's name to "Israel" (meaning "struggles with God").

Stop the story. Ask "Jacob" who he is wrestling with. Open this question up to the group. What do you think this encounter has to do with Jacob's returning to face Esau? Why does "the man" wound Jacob? Why is it sometimes necessary to be wounded in order to be healed? Can you think of a "dark encounter" that you could in fact rename an encounter with God? (Rather than ask for open responses to this last question by the group, consider asking people to share in pairs for a few minutes.)

Genesis 33:1–4: The next morning, Jacob sees Esau coming toward him with four hundred men. Jacob organizes his small band, placing the women servants and their children first, Leah and her children next, and Rachel and her child next. However, rather than sending them ahead, as he had done with his messengers and servants, Jacob goes to the front. As he walks ahead toward Esau, Jacob bows to the ground seven times. Esau runs to meet his brother, embraces him, and kisses him. They both weep.

Stop the story. Remembering the great injustice done to Esau, what do you think enabled Esau to change or "turn"? What do you think Esau needed? What did Jacob need to do? (Past groups have mentioned such matters as *wrestling with one's conscience, encountering God, the role of confession, the need to build trust, and the importance of recognition.*)

Genesis 33:5–17 Esau initially refuses Jacob's gifts but accepts them with Jacob's urging. You may want to read aloud Jacob's response: "If I have found favor in your eyes, accept this gift from me. For to see your face is like seeing the face of God, now that you have received me favorably" (Genesis 33:10). After the two brothers have been reconciled, they do not continue to live together. Each goes his own way. Why?

Application to Life

Open the full story to reflection on healing and reconciliation. Remind participants that there is no "magic wand" to bring about reconciliation. Rather than looking for answers in this story, ask participants to identify the questions Jacob's journey raises for them about the process of reconciliation. Some questions might be the following:

- To what extent is the journey toward forgiveness dependent on the other person or persons?

- How does the healing process begin so that one can let go of anger and hatred?

- Who initiates reconciliation? How important is the struggle with God?

- As agents of reconciliation, how do we recognize the "sacred moments" when change in ourselves and in others may be possible?

Next, hand out pens and paper. Ask participants to work silently and write down the part of the story or the discussion that touched them personally or offered them the greatest insight. After five minutes, form small groups of three, and ask people to share with one another their personal response or things they have learned from the scripture study. (Allow ten minutes.)

SACRED TEXT STUDY #3

Forgiveness and Enemies—Qur'an 60:7–9

Workshop Design

This passage from the Qur'an could be studied in the basic workshop, Day Two, with the sessions on the Problem-Solving or Agreement Stage; in the advanced workshop on community conflict and restoring relationships; or in relationship to Chapter Ten of the *Peace Skills* Manual. It is complementary to the case study "Call to Prayer."

Time

60–90 minutes

Introduction and Background

The following information will provide a helpful introduction to the text, particularly for persons who are not familiar with the Qur'an.

For Muslims who believe that the Qur'an is the word of God revealed to the Prophet Muhammad, all lessons in the Qur'an have a timeless and universal value. At the same time, Muslim scholars emphasize that Qur'anic verses should not be taken out of context, since this can distort their meaning. To understand the lessons derived from a specific verse, we must take into consideration other verses related to the topic; the occasion during the life of the Prophet Muhammad when the verse was revealed, if this is known; and any comments the Prophet may have made interpreting the verse.

The importance of these precautions becomes evident when we hear some people quote Qur'anic verses that seem to indicate that there should be no friendship or cooperation between Muslims and non-Muslims. Consider, therefore, the following verses from Chapter 60 of the Qur'an, which were revealed to the Prophet Muhammad at a time when he and his community were being severely persecuted for their faith. Many Muslims had been exiled from their homes, they had lost their property, and many had lost their lives.

The companions of the Prophet Muhammad narrated that the first verse of Chapter 60 was revealed after one Muslim man tried to pass some information that could hurt the Muslim community to a family member who was actively engaged in fighting the Muslims.

This study (all parts with the exception of the Workshop Design) was prepared by Dr. Ingrid Mattson, professor of Islamic studies and Christian-Muslim relations, Hartford Seminary, Hartford, Connecticut.

Qur'an 60:1

(1) O you who believe, do not take my enemies and your enemies as friends, showing affection towards them, when they have disbelieved in what has come to you of the truth and have driven out the Messenger [Muhammad] and yourselves [from your homes] because you believe in Allah, your Lord....

Qur'an 60:7–9

(7) It may be that Allah will create affection between you and those whom you now consider enemies. Allah is All-Powerful and Allah is Oft-Forgiving, Most Merciful.

(8) Allah does not forbid you, with regard to those who do not fight you because of your faith, nor drive you out of your homes, from dealing kindly and justly with them: for Allah loves those who are just.

(9) Allah only forbids you, with regard to those who fight you for your faith, and drive you out of your homes, and support others in driving you out, from turning to them [for friendship and protection]. It is such as turn to them [in these circumstances], that do wrong.

Questions for Discussion

1. What makes someone an enemy? What might be the significance of the fact that verse 1 uses the phrase, "my enemies and your enemies" while verse 7 uses the phrase "those whom you now consider enemies"?

2. The circumstances under which these verses were revealed indicate that the welfare of the Muslim community was at risk. Internal community solidarity is therefore emphasized. At the same time, the Qur'an is instructing us to differentiate among those who are part of a community we consider to be hostile to us. How do we make such a differentiation?

3. In the Qur'an, God describes Himself using many different terms or "names" such as "the All-Seeing" (*Al-Basir*), "the Creator" (*Al-Fatir*), "the All-Knowing" (*Al-Alim*). In verse 7, Allah describes Himself as "All-Powerful" (*Qadir*), "Oft-Forgiving" (*Ghafur*), "Most Merciful" (*Rahim*). What is the significance of Allah describing Himself here in this manner? What implications do these attributes of God have for how you treat one you consider an enemy?

Application to Life

1. Ask each person in the group to find a quiet place. Ask people to take some time, to close their eyes, and say to themselves the word *enemy*. Ask

them to explore silently the feelings and images that arise as they say this word. Then have them draw a picture of an "enemy." It could be someone they know or an unidentified enemy whom they have never met. Allow two or three minutes for participants to draw their images. Now ask them to set the drawing aside, close their eyes, and say to themselves the words: *affection, kindly, just.* Ask them to explore the feelings and images that arise in their minds as they say these words. Then have them write down ten kind things they might do for a relative or neighbor they feel affectionate toward. Let them keep these pictures and writings private for now.

2. Gather the group together. Ask if participants can recall a time when as a child they had a serious falling out with a friend or a sibling and were later reconciled. How did this reconciliation happen? Now ask if there are individuals in the group who can explain why they now feel, as an adult, that they can help children (their own children or children under their care) resolve conflicts among themselves. What abilities or knowledge do we hope adults have to solve such conflicts that children may be lacking? Now compare our perspective to our conflicts with God's perspective. What abilities or knowledge does God have to help us that we do not have? Perhaps the group would like to recite together the "names" Allah gives Himself in the chapter we are studying: "All-Powerful," "Oft-Forgiving," "Most Merciful."

3. Let everyone now look back privately at the "enemy" pictures. Imagine that this enemy moved in next door. Now imagine, one by one, doing the ten kindnesses for this person. How does that person feel each time you do one of these things? Now draw another picture of the "enemy." Does he or she look any different? In what way? Invite people to share their feelings and drawings in the group.

SACRED TEXT STUDY #4

Justice and Freedom—Preamble to the Constitution of South Africa

Workshop Design

A regular encounter with authoritative or sacred texts continues to be a crucial dimension in South Africa's quest for truth and reconciliation. The National Ethics Engagement Development (NEED) program, launched by the South African Church Community Leadership Trust, devotes part of the NEED curriculum to an exploration of the meaning and implications of these texts. The curriculum includes passages from the Hebrew Scriptures, the Christian New Testament, the Qur'an, the Freedom Charter, the Ubuntu Pledge, and the Preamble to the South African Constitution, featured here. Shared community reflections about these texts and their strategic importance for the continued movement toward a nonracial, nonsexist, democratic South Africa are not only revealing but for many persons have also been life-changing.

This new civic authoritative text has parallels in the United Nations Charter and other national charters. It supplements the basic workshop, Day Two, in a discussion of personal resources for peacebuilding; the "maps of conflict" exercise; and the advanced training analysis of a community conflict.

Time

60–90 minutes

Text

We, the people of South Africa,

Recognize the injustices of our past;

Honor those who suffered for justice and freedom in our land;

Respect those who have worked to build and develop our country; and

Believe that South Africa belongs to all who live in it, united in our diversity.

We therefore, through our freely elected representatives, adopt this Constitution as the supreme law of the Republic so as to—

1. Heal the divisions of the past and establish a society based on democratic values, social justice and fundamental human rights;

These questions and the application exercise were prepared by Margaret Steinegger-Keyser, a South African on the staff of Plowshares Institute, Simsbury, Connecticut.

2. Lay the foundations for a democratic and open society in which government is based on the will of the people and every citizen is equally protected by law;

3. Improve the quality of life of all citizens and free the potential of each person; and

4. Build a united and democratic South Africa able to take its rightful place as a sovereign state in the family of nations.

May God protect our people.

Nkosi Sikelel' iAfrica. *(Xosha, Zulu)*

Morena boloka setjhaba sa heso. *(Sesotho)*

God seën Suid-Afrika. *(Afrikaans)*

God bless South Africa. *(English)*

Mudzimu fhatutshedza Afurika. *(Tshivenda)*

Hosi katekisa Afrika. *(Xitsonga)*

Sample Questions

1. What is the nature of the injustices you have suffered in your country? What injustices have you perpetuated or remained silent about?

2. Who would you set apart to honor for suffering for justice and freedom in your country? Select a well-known and an unknown candidate. By what criteria did you choose them?

3. Who is a South African? What is the basis of citizenship in your country? Provide an example of being united in diversity. Are there limits to the diversity South Africa or any democracy can tolerate?

4. What are the most important foundations of a democratic society? How do you understand "the will of the people"?

5. Does a constitution set the priorities of a nation? How can a constitution become a vehicle to heal past injustices? What other resources are needed to contribute to such healing in a society?

6. What in this preamble speaks to you most powerfully? Identify what you have learned about moral governance of a democracy.

Application Exercises

1. Take fifteen minutes to draft the central elements in an ideal preamble by answering the following questions:

   a. Identify two or three elements that provide moral standards and guidance for each nation in the family of nations that you would like to see in the constitution or an authoritative document

b. Name the right that is under the most threat in your own nation at this time.

c. What specific covenant or promise will you make today to defend or advance this right?

d. What, if anything, might this cost you?

2. Gather in groups of three or four to share your responses. Declare how you will support each other in the defense of rights.

NOTES AND REFERENCES

NOTES

Introduction

1. John Paul Lederach, *Beyond Prescription: New Lenses for Conflict Resolution Training Across Cultures* (Syracuse, N.Y.: Syracuse University Press, 1994). For a further discussion of elicitive training and an excellent set of additional workshop suggestions, refer to Ronald S. Kraybill, "Elicitive Training: Dealing with Conflict Cross-Culturally," in *Track Two* (Cape Town, South Africa: Centre for Conflict Resolution, 1994).

2. In *Pedagogy of the Oppressed* (New York: Herder & Herder, 1972), Brazilian educator Paulo Freire suggests that most educators use a "banking" approach to teaching. The teacher makes a "deposit" of information or knowledge into the student, who is regarded as an "empty vessel." Too often this approach encourages students to be passive and convinces them that they have little to contribute. Freire contrasts "banking" education with "problem posing," which he sees as liberating education—a teaching approach that is open to the possibility of new knowledge and frees teachers and students to become co-learners as they seek to combine their wisdom and experience to resolve a problem.

3. While the basic workshops are tailored to each community, we have found one of the most effective approaches is for communities to sponsor three intensive fourteen-hour workshops over a period of one year. Each workshop involves forty to forty-five civic and religious leaders. Participants in each workshop are invited to join the local multiethnic steering committee and are encouraged to study and share the *Peace Skills* Manual with their constituencies. After a one-day advanced training workshop focused on the Leaders' Guide, some participants become coaches and assistant trainers

for the next workshop and lead trainers for subsequent workshops. For additional information about how these city programs developed, look under "Cities Program" at www.PlowsharesInstitute.com.

In addition to those leaders trained in the United States, more than twenty-five hundred community leaders in Africa, Asia, Europe, and the Caribbean have participated in CCT workshops based on the basic principles of these training materials.

Chapter Two

1. The formal academic use of cases began in North America in 1870 at the Harvard University Law School. Most law schools in the United States later adopted case teaching. Law students were challenged to analyze real recorded situations, rather than memorize legal principles or develop theories about imaginary situations. Along with the analysis of the case, students were expected to decide the best ways to handle the situation and to anticipate sound legal decisions. In 1908, the Harvard University Business School began to use case studies of actual events from the business world to help students develop the skills they needed to analyze situations and make tough decisions. The first systematic attempts to use the case method to teach philosophy and theology were made by a few professors in the 1960s. In 1971, the Association of Theological Schools sponsored the first annual Case Method Institute, working with faculty from the Harvard Business School.

   The Association for Case Teaching (ACT) was formed in 1977 by a group of graduates of the Case Method Institute. ACT publishes an annual journal containing new case studies and sponsors an annual summer workshop on creative teaching skills.

2. Eric Law, *The Wolf Shall Dwell with the Lamb: A Spirituality for Leadership in Multicultural Community* (St. Louis, Mo.: Chalice Press, 1993), offers an insightful analysis of destructive components in multicultural communication.

Chapter Three

1. This discussion and the guidelines that follow are adapted from material developed by Walter Wink and published in *Explorations in Faith: Leaders Guide,* by Robert A. Evans, G. Douglass Lewis, and Marjorie Hall Davis (Bethesda, Md.: Alban Institute, 1981), pp. 3–6. Used by permission. The section "Leading the Study" also draws on Wink's *Transforming Bible Study: A Leaders' Guide,* 2nd ed. (Nashville, Tenn.: Abingdon Press, 1989). Used by permission.

Chapter Four

1. This exercise and the accompanying drawings were created by Ronald S. Kraybill and are described in his essay "Conflict in Groups: The Cross-Stitching Effect," in *Mediation and Facilitation Training Manual: Foundations and Skills for Constructive Conflict Transformation, Fourth Edition*, edited by Carolyn Schrock-Shenk (Akron, Pa.: Mennonite Conciliation Service, 2000), pp. 247–252.

2. The idea that conflict may actually bind a community together originated with the sociologist Lewis Coser, who wrote about this phenomenon in *The Functions of Social Conflict* (New York: Free Press, 1956), pp. 72–80.

Chapter Six

1. This design for this session (all but step 5) was developed with Kathleen Hiyake Chuman, Urban Leadership Institute, Los Angeles.

Chapter Nine

1. The questions, application, and background notes are adapted from material published in Wink, *Transforming Bible Study*, pp. 141–142.

2. These questions are based on a Bible study conducted during a peacebuilding course. They were developed by John Paul Lederach, professor in the Conflict Transformation Program, Eastern Mennonite University. Used by permission. For further discussion of the text and several of the questions, see his book *The Journey Toward Reconciliation* (Scottdale, Pa.: Herald Press, 1999).

REFERENCES

Bonhoeffer, D. "The Ministry of Listening." In *Life Together* (J. Dobbenstein, trans.). New York: HarperCollins, 1954.

Bush, R.A.B., and Folger, J. P. *The Promise of Mediation: Responding to Conflict Through Empowerment and Recognition.* San Francisco: Jossey-Bass, 1994.

Wink, W. *Transforming Bible Study: A Leaders' Guide.* (2nd ed.) Nashville, Tenn.: Abingdon Press, 1989.

Zimmer, H. *The King and the Corpse: Tales of the Soul's Conquest of Evil.* Princeton, N.J.: Princeton University Press, 1993.

FURTHER READING

Teaching Resources

Lederach, J. P. *Preparing for Peace: Conflict Transformation Across Cultures.* New York: Syracuse University Press, 1995. Recognizing the dangers of seeking to teach people in one culture the skills for responding to conflict that have been developed in another, this book describes an "elicitive" approach to training that takes seriously the knowledge and skills in responding to conflict that are present in every cultural context.

Lynn, L. E. *Teaching and Learning with Cases: A Guidebook.* New York: Chatham House, 1999. Readable and comprehensive presentation of basic principles of case preparation, teaching, and writing.

Mock, R. *The Roleplay Book: 41 Hypothetical Situations.* (2nd ed.) Akron, Pa.: Mennonite Conciliation Service, 1997. Contains role-plays relevant for a variety of audiences and teaching situations.

Schrock-Shenk, C. (eds.). *Mediation and Facilitation Training Manual: Foundations and Skills for Constructive Conflict Transformation.* (4th ed.) Akron, Pa.: Mennonite Conciliation Service, 2000. An excellent compendium of articles, training exercises, and concrete methodological approaches to a wide variety of mediation and facilitation issues and situations.

Vella, J. *Learning to Teach, Learning to Listen.* San Francisco: Jossey-Bass, 1994; Vella, J. *Training Through Dialogue.* San Francisco: Jossey-Bass, 1996. Vella's books are about training in general, but they describe learning methods that are essential for training in peacebuilding. They assist in design and delivery of workshops that take seriously the knowledge and insights of participants and empower them to build on the resources they bring to the topic of study.

THE AUTHORS

ALICE FRAZER EVANS was educated at Agnes Scott College, University of Edinburgh, and University of Wisconsin. She is the director of writing and research at Plowshares Institute and senior fellow at the Centre for Conflict Resolution in Cape Town, South Africa. A prolific case writer, she has focused on the development of international case studies, with special attention to the use of cases in conflict transformation training. Alice Evans is the founding executive director of an international association for case teaching. She is the co-author and editor of a number of books on global issues including *Christian Ethics: A Case Method Approach, Pastoral Theology from a Global Perspective,* and *Pedagogies for the Non-Poor.* She is a co-national director of a project on empowering for reconciliation with justice for which she developed curriculum material for civic and religious leaders in ten pilot project cities from Los Angeles to Philadelphia. Alice has taught, consulted, and trained case writers in workshops in Africa, Asia, Europe, Latin America, and North America. She is an elder and lay leader in the United Presbyterian Church. Her current teaching, research, and writing focus on U.S. cities, China, Indonesia, East Timor, and east and southern Africa.

ROBERT A. EVANS studied at Yale and the Universities of Edinburgh, Berlin, and Basel. He received his doctorate from Union Theological Seminary in New York. He is the author, co-author, editor of a dozen books, including *Globalization of Theological Education, Case Book for Christian Living,* and *Human Rights: A Dialogue Between the First and Third Worlds.* An ordained Presbyterian pastor, Bob Evans served as a professor in universities and seminaries in New York, Chicago, Uganda, Fiji, and Hartford. He currently serves as a senior fellow at the Centre for Conflict Resolution in Cape Town, South Africa. Bob is the founder and executive director of Plowshares Institute, which is committed to education, research, and dialogue for a more just, sustainable, and peaceful world community. He leads intensive traveling seminars for government, business, and religious leaders from Africa, Asia, and Latin America. He conducts national and international seminars on skills training in community conflict transformation on five continents. Bob co-directed with Alice Frazer Evans a pilot program for the Pew, Ford, and Kellogg Foundations in Philadelphia and Los Angeles on empowering for reconciliation with justice. This project, which has expanded to eight other cities in North America, equips multiethnic teams of religious and civic leaders to be proactive intervenors in community conflict situations. Bob and Alice Evans are currently developing projects in conflict transformation and sustainable development in East Timor, Hong Kong, Indonesia, Kenya, Uganda, and Zimbabwe.

RONALD S. KRAYBILL holds a bachelor's degree from Goshen College, a master's degree in divinity from Harvard Divinity School, and a doctorate in religious studies from the University of Cape Town. From 1979 to 1988, Kraybill was founding director of the Mennonite Conciliation Service based in Akron, Pennsylvania, and in this capacity worked with conflicts in family, community, business, neighborhood, and congregational settings and trained a large number of people in mediation skills. From 1989 to 1995, he served as director of training at the Centre for Conflict Resolution in Cape Town, South Africa. During the years of the South African political transition, he trained local, regional, and national leadership in negotiation and mediation skills and served as a training adviser to the National Peace Accord. Since 1995 Kraybill has been an associate professor in the Conflict Transformation Program at Eastern Mennonite University in Harrisonburg, Virginia, where he and his colleagues work with a network of partner organizations in the United States, Latin America, Africa, Asia, and Europe. From August 1999 to June 2000, Kraybill served as a visiting professor at the Henry Martyn Institute, an international center for interreligious dialogue and reconciliation in Hyderabad, India. In addition to many published essays, he has written *Repairing the Breach: Ministering in Community Conflict*, co-edited with Lynn Buzzard *Mediation: A Reader*, and edited *Training Manual for Conflict Transformation Skills*.

ABOUT PLOWSHARES INSTITUTE

PLOWSHARES INSTITUTE WAS FOUNDED in 1981 to address systemic issues of injustice through education, research, and service. A nonprofit agency in partnership with an international advisory council and collaborative agencies on five continents, the Institute staff designs and implements pilot projects to promote a more just, sustainable, and peaceful world society. Pilot projects have included the Citizens of the World, Empowering for Reconciliation with Justice, Globalization of Theological Education, and Community Conflict Transformation (CCT).

The goal of community conflict transformation programs is to provide mediation skills training and curriculum material to equip civic, religious, and business leaders to work together in building just and more harmonious communities. For the past decade Plowshares staff members have been working with government and community leaders in Asia, Africa, and in ten North American cities from Los Angeles to Hartford in proactive approaches to community conflict. Multiethnic and multicultural teams of mediators trained in these programs have helped transform communities dealing with problems from community policing to public education. Workshop participants have also become trainers, equipping additional local leaders with mediation and transformation skills in East Timor, Hong Kong, Indonesia, Kenya, North America, South Africa, Uganda, and Zimbabwe.

Plowshares directors, Robert A. Evans and Alice Frazer Evans, are consultants and lead seminars for civic, business, academic, religious, and military leaders on five continents. The Evanses began developing a model for international immersion seminars in 1975. More than forty Plowshares seminars have brought together community and religious and leaders from North America with colleagues in Africa, Asia, Australia, Central Europe, and Latin America. The seminars not only build mutually beneficial international relationships, they also have a proven record of energizing participants to apply what they learn overseas to address local problems. Plowshares directly supports with volunteer service and funds a number of non-profit organizations in the developing world which share its vision.

The Evanses were founding members of the Association for Case Teaching and its co-executive directors for more than twenty-five years. Because of its potential for cooperative learning and for empowering people to draw on their own skills and experience to resolve dilemmas, the case method is a foundational pedagogy for Plowshares training in community conflict transformation.

Plowshares research, designed to share insights and promote the goals of pilot projects, is published in the form of case studies, articles, and a dozen books. The books include *Changing the Way Seminaries Teach; Christian Ethics: A Case Method Approach; The Globalization of Theological Education; Human Rights: A Dialogue Between the First and Third Worlds; Pastoral Theology from a Global Perspective;* and *Pedagogies for the Non-Poor.*

Peace Skills in Action: A Video for Community Conflict Transformation (CCT) Training and Interpretation

The twenty-minute video dramatically presents the need, vision, background, content, and consequences of Community Conflict Transformation training. This proactive approach to conflict intervention is illustrated by images of individuals and communities engaged in the training. The video also includes presentations on the impact of conflict transformation by mediators and trainers from Africa, Asia, and North America. This engaging video is designed to be used as an instrument to recruit workshop participants, to secure funding for the training, to clarify the approach, and to show CCT's global and local applications.

The video is available from Plowshares Institute, P.O. Box 243, Simsbury, CT 06070. Phone: 860/651–4304; Fax: 860/651–4305; e-mail: Plowshares@ hartsem.edu. Please consult the Plowshares's Web site for additional information: www.plowsharesinstitute.com.

ABOUT THE CONFLICT TRANSFORMATION PROGRAM

WELCOMING PEOPLE from all parts of the world and all religious traditions, the CTP is an outgrowth of the centuries-old Mennonite peace tradition rooted in values of nonviolence, social justice, public service, reconciliation, personal wholeness, and appreciation for diversity. Established in 1994 at Eastern Mennonite University in Harrisonburg, Virginia, the program builds on the extensive experience of Mennonites in the areas of disaster response, humanitarian relief, socio-economic development, conciliation, trauma healing, and restorative justice in exploring peaceful and creative responses to conflict.

Three closely related initiatives make up the CTP. An academic program offers a forty-two-credit-hour master's degree in conflict transformation for residential and limited-residential students, as well as a fifteen-hour-graduate certificate. Both are designed for persons with experience in conflict transformation or related areas, such as humanitarian assistance, community services, restorative justice, advocacy, human rights, or development activities, and who seek additional preparation in the field of conflict transformation. Students are encouraged to concentrate in one of six areas: conflict transformation and peacebuilding, restorative justice, mediation and facilitation, conflict transformation and the congregation, conflict transformation and organizational leadership, or conflict transformation and education. Since the work of peacebuilding is demanding, students are also encouraged to develop ethical, emotional, and spiritual resources to sustain them in long-term work in stressful situations. In 2000, seventy students from every region of the world enrolled and were taught by six core faculty and a larger number of adjunct faculty.

The Institute for Justice and Peacebuilding (IJP) is the applied practice and research component of the Conflict Transformation Program. It provides direct services in peacebuilding in the form of trainings, consultancies, peace-process design, conciliation, mediation, and action-oriented research to religious, academic, intergovernmental, and community organizations worldwide. IJP is staffed by associates who, as practitioner/scholars, have broad experience as educators and trainers in conflict transformation and as practitioners of peacebuilding. With extensive experience in diverse cultural environments, they are in the forefront of culturally contextualized approaches to the training and practice of conflict transformation. Through links with strategic partners in Africa, Asia, and Latin America and with practitioners engaged in peacebuilding worldwide, the Institute for Justice and Peacebuilding provides a connection between current practice and advances in theory and concept.

The Summer Peacebuilding Institute is held annually in May and June for academic and non-academic participants who seek an intensive training experience with diverse colleagues from around the world. Participants choose from among fifteen seven-day courses in conflict transformation, mediation and facilitation, trauma healing, restorative justice, and other topics. In 2000, 141 participants attended from forty-five countries and seventeen U.S. states, representing seven religious traditions and twenty Christian denominations, with almost equal numbers of women and men. Participants were affiliated with religious and humanitarian agencies, with non-governmental, governmental, and intergovernmental organizations, as well as with peacebuilding and conflict transformation programs, restorative justice organizations, and academic institutions.

For more information and access to additional related Web sites, visit the Conflict Transformation Program Web site at: www.emu.edu/ctp/ctp.html.

Conflict Transformation Program, Eastern Mennonite University, Harrisonburg, VA, 22802. Phone: (540) 432–4490; Fax: (540) 432–4449; email: ctprogram@emu.edu.

INDEX

195